THE AGENCY FOR ALL THINGS SPECTRAL

Published in the UK by Sweet Cherry Publishing Limited, 2025

Unit 36, Vulcan House, Vulcan Road,
Leicester LE5 3EF, United Kingdom

Unit 31, The Pottery, Bakers Point,
Pottery Road, Dún Laoghaire,
Dublin A96 EV18, Ireland

SWEET CHERRY and associated logos are trademarks and/or
registered trademarks of Sweet Cherry Publishing Limited.

2 4 6 8 10 9 7 5 3 1

ISBN: 978-1-80263-694-9

The Agency for All Things Spectral:
The Case of Dr Dust

Text by Samuel J Haplin
Illustrations by Laura Borio

www.sweetcherrypublishing.com

Printed and bound in the UK using 100% renewable electricity
at CPI Group (UK) Ltd.

MIX
Paper | Supporting
responsible forestry
FSC® C171272

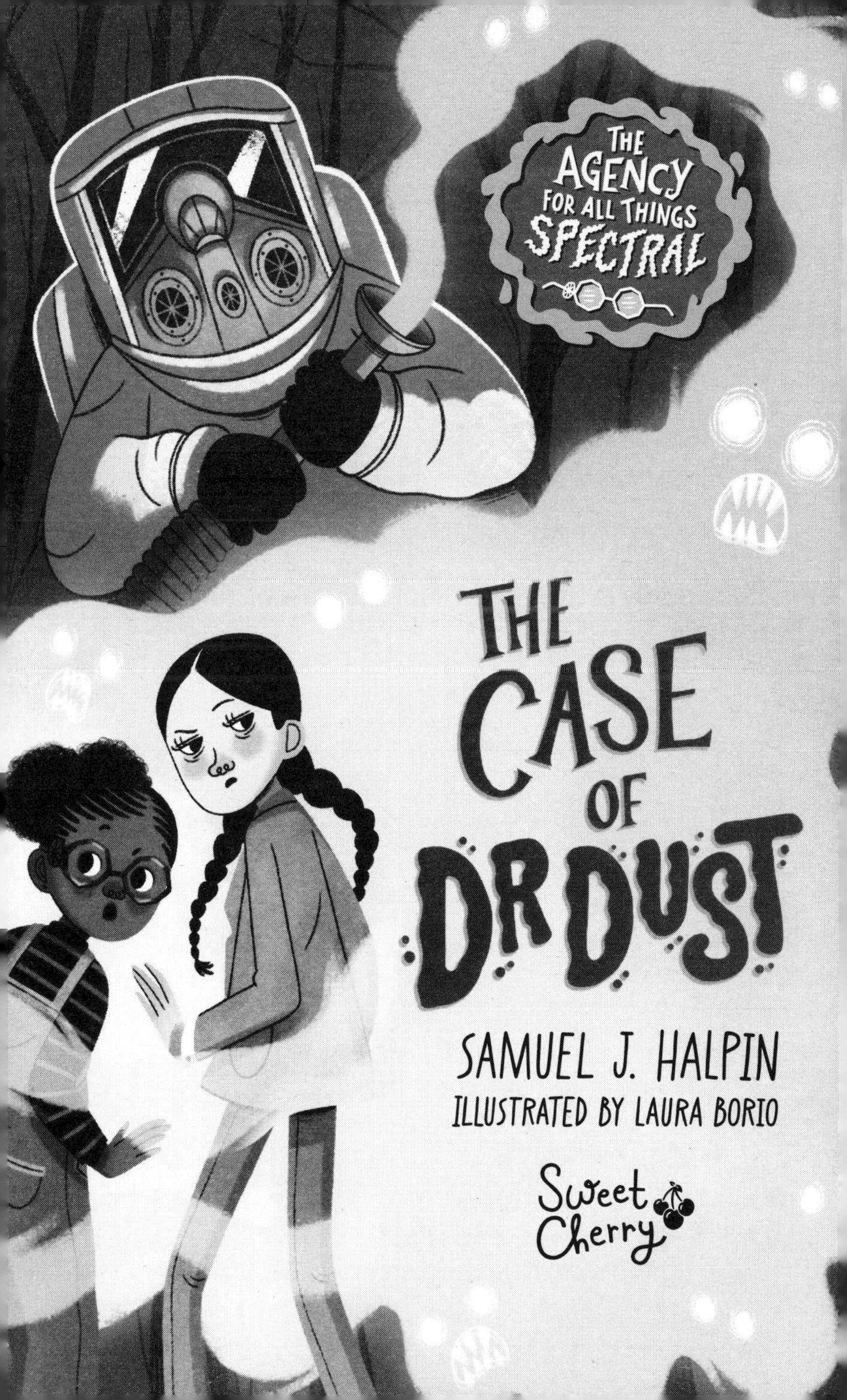

THE AGENCY FOR ALL THINGS SPECTRAL

THE CASE OF DR DUST

SAMUEL J. HALPIN

ILLUSTRATED BY LAURA BORIO

Sweet Cherry

CHAPTER 1

THE GOLDFISH

It started with screaming. Terrible, awful, call-the-armed-forces type screaming.

'Billy!' Both Mums flew through the door as from my bed, I gazed in horror at the fish tank.

Mum One (Mum) was hunting frantically for what had made me scream and carrying my little brother Jude in one arm. Mum Two (Ma) was wielding a golf club (9-iron, if you're familiar).

'Oh. Right.' Mum said flatly when she
caught sight of the fish tank. It was a cloudy,
poisonous green. And on top of it my goldfish,
Hepzibah, was floating upside down.

It was a Monday. I tried to just pretend everything would be better in the morning, but little did I know that the very next day things would only get worse. Because at the Mums' antique shop, the man with the flashy smile and the little briefcase came in again to try offer them more money to sell it.

Mum said the flashy little man is from a big company called Bullham's Developments that wants to buy up all the shops in our town so they can knock them down and build a shopping centre on top. Ma then said she'd quite like to knock down the flashy little man and build a shop on top of him just to see how he liked it. And Mum hissed, 'Not in front of the children,' so Ma said, 'Why not! It's pretty clear to me we've raised a … goldfish murderer!'

The shock rang through me like a gong.
And I didn't want to admit it then, but
looking back now I think Ma was right.
Mums had asked me *three* times to clean
Hepzibah's tank and I just kept putting
it off.

Had I killed her? I thought. *Was it really
me who killed sweet, darling, sometimes
quite smelly Hepzibah?*

After Ma said that, I went away for a bit
to my tree house and my little head got to
cooking up a plan.

*If you could just find a way to make
some money, then you could always buy
another goldfish that looks exactly the
same, call her Hepzibah, and you wouldn't
have to feel guilty anymore.*

I let the plan simmer for a bit, as I dangled my legs out the opening of the treehouse.

Ma built it for me a few years back, and it even looks out at the park behind our house. The park is just a scraggly green field with a lonely swing set right in the middle. But as I watched the chains swaying in the wind, the plan began to soften up nicely in my head.

Oh, it was good alright. A plan which destined me for greatness. For glory. Such glory that my name, Billy Hazel Duggery, would be printed on bottles for years to come with a picture of me on the front. Maybe doing a thumbs up.

But there was more in the air than just a plan brewing. There was trouble. Some pretty spectacular, Big-Ben-sized trouble.

* * *

'Never in all my years, did I think our daughter would turn out … a … *con artist*!'

Ma finished off in a loud whisper, as if someone might hear her.

If I were her, I'd be more worried about people seeing me wearing those tartan golf trousers of hers.

'What were you thinking, Billy?' Mum sighed disappointedly waving the empty lemonade bottle at me.

I didn't know what they were so upset about. All I'd done was get the brilliant idea to set up a lemonade stand to raise enough money to buy Hepzibah II. Only, all the lemonades I'd concocted tasted terrible. I tried adding some cayenne pepper and just a pinch of fish flakes to give it a unique selling point, but nothing seemed to work. So instead, I poured a bottle of lemonade Mum had bought from the supermarket into a jug and added some mint I found growing out of the pavement to make it look to make it look homemade.

We were having a sudden hot spell at the end of the summer holidays. And I did a roaring trade and made £6.30. People kept asking me for the recipe. But I shook my head and said, 'It's an old family secret. So if I told you, I'm afraid I'd have to kill you.'

'That's *lying*, Billy.' Mum told me. 'You can't trick people into thinking it's homemade and then charge them thirty pence! You need to find everyone on the street who bought your lemonade and refund them their money. And don't give me that look!'

It was the most humiliating day in all nine years of my life.

'No wonder the boys were so hyperactive!' Mr Shah who has twins told me when I knocked on his door. Behind him, I could see one of the twins climbing up a bookshelf and the other swinging on a curtain like it was a jungle vine. But I don't know what *he* was so upset about.

His twins are always like that.

I apologised my way miserably down the street: knocking on each door, explaining and refunding until, finally, I got to Mrs Benjamin's. She collects spoons and lives in the house next to ours. I knocked. Then knocked again. But there was no answer. And when I leaned over her climbing rosebush and peered in through the window it was all dark inside.

As I plodded back to our house, I stopped to scoop up our mail, which for some reason *never* stays in our letterbox and always seems to be scattered over the footpath. I think we have a secret postal nemesis, but Mum just says our postman should be called Frisby.

Once I'd stacked the mail on the kitchen counter, I popped Mrs Benjamin's 30p in a purse next to my bed to keep it safe. Then settled into a suitable funk in the corner of my room, gazing every so often at Hepzibah's empty tank. Hepzibah had been a birthday gift from my best friend Dev. And when I thought about it, I realised maybe that was *really* what all this was about. Because Dev hadn't been talking to me all summer.

I haven't always called him Dev. I've got many names for him: Dev. Devilled Egg. Devon. Dorset, (it was about *here* he made the mistake of telling me he'd once been to Tasmania). Tassie *Dev*il. Tazzy Dev. Tazzy. Devvy Taz. Then finally Dev again because he likes his real name best.

We'd had a fight at school because we both got in trouble for something I'd done. I tried explaining to our Principal Mr Eugene, but he wouldn't hear a word of it.

And as I sat in my room reviewing my criminal record of goldfish murder in the third degree and lemonade fraud in the second, Mum came in with an addition to the list:

'Dev's Mum called and said they can't have you over tomorrow anymore. Family stuff,' Mum told me softly. But I knew it was because Dev just didn't want to see me.

'So,' Mum smiled flatly, 'you're going to have to come into the shop with me tomorrow.'

Mum usually runs the antique shop, which is called *Past Life*. And Ma has a little workshop in our back garden where she restores furniture.

I had a little cry that night in bed. Mostly because I felt sorry for myself, and also because of Hepzibah, whose funeral we'd had that day.

And although I woke up feeling exactly the same: pancake flat and court-convicted guilty; little did I know that in just a few short hours I was going to find something *exceptionally* strange.

Something that would change my life, and Stony Brook as I knew it, forever.

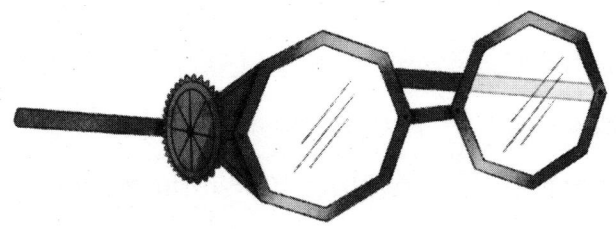

CHAPTER 2

A SUSPICIOUS BURIAL

The antique shop smelt musty and glossy. Like a charity clothes bin mixed with varnish. There were hardly any customers. Mum had me untangling vintage Christmas lights in the back.

'Beef patty from the bakery?' Mum smiled sweetly.

She took the money from the till.

I thought about paying for it myself, because we hadn't had any customers that day, but then remembered that all I had was 30p and that was Mrs Benjamin's.

'Custard Twists make life so much better, don't they?' Mum squinted happily, unfurling hers like a roll of bubble gum and eating it bit by bit.

I was good all afternoon and didn't break one thing, which must be some sort of record in a shop that's as crammed with janky old junk as Mums'. At five p.m. Mum went out the front to take down the awning and start closing up.

I tied up the bag in the wastepaper bin and carried it out the back.

Behind the antique shop was an alley, lined with packing crates and whiffy bins. Between two of the buildings was an old worksite. It was mostly piles of rubble, rusty scaffolding and a cement mixer full of water. I never really liked hanging out near it because it was a little spooky.

Opening our green rubbish skip I swung the bag inside and dusted off my hands.

But an unusual, rhythmic sound made my ears prick up.

TCHK! TCHK! TCHK! TCHK!

I stopped. Listening.

TCHK! TCHK! TCHK!

Ignoring my better judgement, I stepped across the street, peering into the derelict building site as the black and yellow barrier tape drifted raggedly in the wind.

'Hello?' I called out.

The sound just kept going.

Maybe it was a bird?

I hid behind the cement mixer and craned my neck to get a better view. A very thin man, with pencil-lead circles under his eyes, seemed to be digging a hole next to a pile of building rubble.

I stayed very still. Watching.

If I was any judge, and given he had a beanie pulled down over his ears on what was a reasonably warm day, the very thin man did *not* want to be seen.

He knelt down, glanced nervously around, and removing something wrapped in plastic from his pocket he dropped it in the hole.

What was it?

He began working quickly, scooping

handfuls of dirt back on top until it was flat again and taking the shovel patted down the burial site.

Maybe it was shady money? A wad of cash?

With a scuffle, the suspicious man threw down the shovel, slipped beneath the barrier tape and speed-walked down the alley.

Who was he?

Once I heard his nervous little footsteps patter into the distance, I slinked across the building site.

Snatching up the shovel, I began to dig, quick, sharp jabs into the soil until there was a plasticky rustle.

And kneeling down, I clawed aside the dirt as the little parcel came into view.

I turned it in my hands.

It was a black glasses case like the ones Mum kept her sunnies in. Except posher.

'Billy? Everything OK?' I heard Mum

calling out, and I jammed the glasses case into my pocket, just in time to see written in silver letters on the front:

SPECTRACLES
(with adjustable wavelength focus)

When we got home that evening, I tried calling Dev. He would love the story about the suspicious man at the building site.

'Choudhary's Squeaky Clean Carpet Cleaning Machine Hire, Manisha speaking?' Dev's older sister, Manisha, answered the phone. Dev's parents have a carpet cleaning machine hire business they run from home.

'It's Billy.'

'Dev's not here. He's out with a friend,' she blurted out.

'You don't even know what I was going to ask yet?!' I snapped.

'Then what do you want?'

She was always like this.

I coughed. 'Is err, Dev around?'

She hung up.

'You OK?' Mum asked me as I put the phone down. As I opened my mouth to answer, there was a wail from Jude's bedroom just as Ma sank into the sofa.

'SHOTGUN NOT!' Ma shouted, so that she wouldn't have to lull noisy, dribbly Jude back to sleep. Mum rolled her eyes, launching herself off the sofa towards Jude's nursery. Ma switched on the telly. I went up to my room and arranged my beanbag facing the window, which is where I usually put it so I can feel sorry for myself.

My room is actually quite nice. I have a
planetarium projector which I like switching
on at night and a big Elton John poster
above my desk. My favourite song is *I'm Still
Standing* but I like the way he dresses best.
I'd already decided when I get a proper job
that the first thing, I'll buy is a sequined
baseball uniform with 'BILLY' across the
front.

In my beanbag I cosied up and let out
a little sigh. I really thought I was Dev's
only friend. We've been besties since
Kindergarten. But maybe it's just selfish of
me to want Dev all to myself?

He could bake *anything*. But his raspberry
brownies with white chocolate chip were
to die for. They were a banquet-for-one. A
meal-in-a-mouthful.

A wave of sadness came over me so quickly that I decided I had to distract myself. Reaching into my pocket I pulled out the glasses case I'd seen that man burying.

I read the top again.

SPECTRACLES
(with new adjustable wavelength focus)

Inside the black velvet case was a pair of the most unusual looking spectacles I'd ever seen. They were silver and octagonal. With a small knob on the side like the ones they had on the microscopes at school.

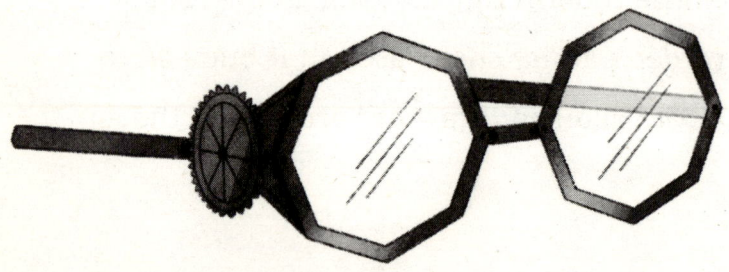

Dev would LOVE these. I knew straight away that I could use them to dress up as Elton John again for Halloween. But it was only when I lifted them out from the case, I found a small slip of paper glued inside:

WARNING: NOT TO BE USED BY
THOSE OF A NERVOUS DISPOSITION

I put them on at once.

Peering down into the dark street, I slowly turned the wavelength knob on the right, hoping that what I could see through the spectacles was as unusual as I'd hoped. But it wasn't. All I could see was Mrs Benjamin whose rubbish tin was rolling down her garden path as she chased it. It bumped to a halt, and she threw her arms up in the air and stormed back inside her dark house.

I got out of the beanbag and walked around my room, adjusting the wavelength knob as I went. Eventually I sat down at the mirror opposite my bed.

I looked brilliant in the spectacles, though I said so myself. Maybe I just had one of those faces that suited octagons?

As I was admiring my reflection, I noticed Hepzibah, my dead goldfish, lazily swimming upside down through the room behind me.

I thought, *Oh, hey Hepzibah.*

Then I thought. *Hold on.*

Then I went. *But you're ... not ... hang on–*

And I fainted.

CHAPTER 3

MRS BENJAMIN'S 30P

When I woke up, I was lying on the ground.
No one had found me and nursed me back
to health. I was upstairs having fainted, and
Ma was probably cracking open the Bourbon
Creams and watching *Antiques Roadshow*.

The spectacles had come off when
I fell. My eyes darted around the room.
To my relief there were no dead fish.
Until I stupidly put those spectacles
on again, and lo and behold there was

Hepzibah, just inches from my nose, floating upside down as if she were underwater.

It's revenge, I told myself. *She's come back from beyond the iPhone-box-grave we buried her in to haunt me for my negligence.*

'Wh-what do you *want*?!' I hissed. But Hepzibah just did little loops with her fins and opened and closed her mouth.

I flung off the glasses, my heart pounding and Hepzibah vanished once more.

What in the name of Mac and Cheese was going on?

I held my arms out, watching my hands shaking.

Why could I see my goldfish, my DEAD goldfish, through these spectacles?

Something tickled the back of my neck and scrambling to my feet, I crouched defensively.

'I'm SORRY, alright?!' I shouted, hoping Hepzibah would somehow be able to understand me. 'I didn't mean to neglect you. There was just a really good episode of *Kids in the Park* on, and I meant to clean your tank after but ...'

Silence.

I put the spectacles back in their case and turned it over in my hands. There was more silver writing on the bottom.

Proudly handcrafted by
BERNARD SOLOMON'S SPECIALIST SPECTACLES
10% Discount when you use referral code:
BERNIE10

I needed to tell someone. But Mums couldn't know, otherwise I'd have to tell them how I'd found them. And besides,

Mums would *never* believe me. I remember Ma once saying that it was always people who were a bit eccentric that said they saw ghosts. I needed Dev. Devilled Egg. Good old trusty Tazzy-Dev. And if he wasn't going to take my calls, then I'd have to resort to doorstepping him.

Dev and I met in year one. When we were being allocated desks, our teacher Miss Spiggot put me beside Timmy Lawrence at the back and started teaching us.

'Pssst! Oi!' I distracted Timmy. 'I have two Mums; how many do you have?'

'One.' Timmy smiled, and I thought, *Brilliant. My first friend.*

'Do you have a bendy ruler?' Timmy asked.

'No.' I said. 'But I have an empty pen you can shoot things through. Look.'

'Billy!' Miss Spiggot snapped. 'I'm going to have to move you. You're distracting people. Come sit next to Louisa Pestle.'

Louisa Pestle had the look of a Straight A student about her. Even her hair looked Straight A.

'Psst! Luisa!' I hissed. 'Look at this.'

I showed her my pencil sharpener which was in the shape of a nose. You could sharpen your pencils inside the nostril.

'Miss!' Louisa's hand shot up. 'Billy's distracting again.'

'Billy.' Miss Spiggot sighed. 'Are we going to keep doing this all day? Move up here next to Dev Choudhary.'

I gathered my things and slouched into the empty desk. Dev was the mousiest-looking person I'd ever seen. I did not have high hopes.

Miss Spiggot went on teaching, and I went on with my distracting. Dev didn't seem to be bothered. He just kept focus. The more I poked and prodded and shot paper-planes at him, the less he seemed to react.

And the more interested in this little person I became.

By break time, I'd already eaten all my lunch, so I just kept on talking, and looking hungry as Dev spread his banquet out on a tea towel.

But as I blabbered on, Dev produced a muffin.

I remember my heart skipping two full beats.

This was no ordinary muffin. It was one of the most exquisite muffins I'd ever seen. Buttery and sticky and so packed with blueberries, it looked like it was going to explode.

There must have been a longing glint in my eye because Dev (who was just about to take a bite) said to me: 'D-do you want half?'

'Oh … no…' I resisted politely. 'That's your lunch.'

But I must have looked particularly ravenous because then Dev said:

'No, it's fine … really.' He broke the muffin in two. 'I bake them all the time.'

That was it. Dev brought in two of everything after that. We've been inseparable since. And it taught me a valuable life lesson: generosity and a little sweetness are the foundation stones of the greatest friendships.

'He doesn't want to talk to you.' Manisha folded her arms when I knocked the next morning. I'd spent a sleepless night with a phantom fish floating somewhere around my room.

'It's urgent.' I whispered. 'Tell him that ... he's won a baking competition or something. And that I'm delivering the prize.'

Manisha rolled her eyes and called out. 'DEV. There's someone at the door for you. They're saying you've won a prize.'

Looking back, this was the wrong thing to do. Because when Dev skidded to the front door, he was even *more* disappointed to see it was only me.

'Oh. It's you,' Dev muttered, his apron sprinkled with powdered sugar.

'Please.' I begged. 'Dev. Just. Hear me out. It's important. Get-Buckingham-Palace-on-the-line type important.'

'Can't you two have your argument somewhere else?' Manisha shouted from the living room.

Dev rolled his eyes and reluctantly let me in.

'What is it?' he sighed, once we were safely in his room.

'These spectacles.' I told him, passing him the case. 'They're magic. A weird man tried to *bury* them at the old building site behind Mums' antique shop yesterday. When I looked through them, I saw Hepzibah.'

'So?' Dev asked.

'Hepzibah *died*.' I revealed dramatically.

'You *killed* Hepzibah?!'

'No!' I insisted. 'Well … I didn't *mean* to.'

Dev squinted.

'Is this just your way of trying to talk to me again, Billy? Because I'm not ready yet. It's your fault I got in trouble. Mum thinks you're a bad influence. And I don't want to keep getting detention.'

'Dev,' I pleaded. 'I know you're mad at me. And I'm sorry. But there was no one else I trust.'

Dev sighed, and putting the spectacles on he looked around the room.

'Looks normal to me,' he shrugged.

'Adjust the wavelength focus,' I told him.

He adjusted.

'Nothing,' he snorted.

'I don't understand!' I sighed putting them on myself. 'I PROMISE you I could see Hepzibah. She was floating upside down as if she was ... a ghost.'

'I'm not getting involved in another one of your schemes.' Dev snapped. '*You* might like making trouble. But I don't. All you ever do is think about yourself.'

Dev asked me to leave.

He'd never asked me to leave before. His mum has. But he's always begged me to stay.

I felt cold and empty and hopeless as I hurried back down the street.

I *couldn't* have imagined it, could I?

Getting the Spectracles sulkily out of my pocket, I pushed them up my nose, hoping to catch sight of Hepzibah in my bedroom window to prove I hadn't gone barmy. But the only person I could see was Mrs Benjamin blowing frustratedly on the creeping rosebush outside her house.

'Hi, Mrs Benjamin.' I waved miserably. 'Your roses got aphids again? I've got 30p I need to give you back. Long story. But I'll get it now.'

Mrs Benjamin stared at me. A mixture of horror and shock plastered across her face.

It was unnerving. Was she really that angry about the lemonade? Bolting upstairs, I took her 30p from my purse and scurried back down.

'Billy,' Ma's voice came suspiciously from her workshop as I headed down our front path. 'What are you up to?'

'Returning Mrs Benjamin her 30p.' I told

her hiding the spectacles in the front pocket of my dungarees.

'Oh.' Ma said gravely brushing some sawdust off her apron. 'We should have told you, love. We wanted to choose the right moment, because ... well ... we thought it might upset you.'

I shifted on the spot, wishing Ma would get on with it.

'Mrs Benjamin's daughter called and told us that her mother took a fall last week and ... well, I'm afraid she died.'

CHAPTER 4

THE OTHERS

I stayed in my room the rest of that day lying on the floor.

My thoughts kept tripping over each other.

What if ... but how can ... maybe it's ...

Pulling out the spectacles, I put them back on as I lay there.

Hepzibah was floating right above me. But this time, instead of panicking, I watched her.

'Hey there,' I whispered. From where I lay, she looked the right way up. Hepzibah's mouth opened and closed. I tried to touch her, but my trembling fingers slipped right through her. And for a moment her gold colours shimmered transparently.

I swallowed, steeling my nerves.

'A-are you a g-ghost, Hepzibah?'

Hepzibah did a little loop, her tail swirling beautifully.

How I wished I'd just listened to Mums and cleaned Hepzibah's tank.

Maybe that's why I was seeing ghosts? Because of the terrible wrongs I'd done. Mrs Benjamin was a kind old lady, but she did get snippy at me the other week when I decapitated one of her lilies with a skipping rope. (I was trying to lasso the letter box.)

Was that why she'd come back from the dead to haunt me? Or was it over the 30p I still owed her? Maybe if I just returned it to her, she'd vanish?

There was only one way to find out.

But stupidly. VERY stupidly. I didn't work up the courage to go over to her house again until after dinner.

When *night* was setting in.

The climbing roses were bone-coloured in the streetlight. And when I peered in through the window, the house was completely dark.

I scooted around to the back where Mrs Benjamin kept a key under the cactus. She'd told me this when she went away to see her grandkids and I'd put food out for her cat, Algebra.

I put on the spectacles. Then with a deep, uncertain breath, I unlocked the door.

It smelled musty.

'H-hello?' I called.

There was a thud from the front of the house, followed by a muttering.

For a moment, I was so close to belting it out of there. But if a little courage and 30p was all it took to get rid of Mrs Benjamin's ghost for good, then I had to do it.

I crept down the corridor and as I peered into the dim living room I saw her, glowing faintly, like old glow-in-the-dark paint.

She was on all fours. The remote for the TV was on the floor and she was ... blowing on it.

'M-Mrs Benjamin?' I stuttered, my fingers gripping the doorway. She almost toppled backwards in shock.

'B-B-Billy?' she gasped. 'Y-you can *see* me?'

I nodded. '*And* hear you.'

'But I thought …' she whispered in amazement, 'I thought *no one* could see me. I died, you know. Last week.'

My nerves began to gather themselves inside of me. Mrs Benjamin was as shocked that I could see her as I was. I explained where the spectacles had come from. About Hepzibah and what it was they seemed to do. Finally, I admitted to her about the lemonade and the 30p.

She snorted. 'Goodness, Billy. I think it would take a little more than 30p to make me linger on this earth.'

I popped the coins on her coffee table, just in case.

'Then what *do* you want?' I asked her,

lifting the spectacles up and down off my
nose, making Mrs Benjamin vanish and
reappear.

'I'd like the telly switched on for a start.
I've been trying to push the power button on
that wretched remote all day.'

I picked up the remote and turned the TV
on for her.

'Lovely,' Mrs Benjamin smiled. 'I can't
touch anything except the floor you see.' She
moved her hand through the lamp behind
her. 'But I discovered that if I blow very, very
hard then it can move things a little. That's
why the remote was on the floor. I knocked
it off the coffee table, but I didn't have
enough lung power to hit the power button.'

I thought for a second.

'So ... you can go through walls?'

'Yes,' Mrs Benjamin said, walking through the wall to the kitchen and then back in behind me. 'And I worked out that if I walk through people. Hang on, I'll show you ...'

Mrs Benjamin walked straight through me. I caught a glimpse of her glowing ribcage, followed by the overwhelming desire to yawn.

So, I yawned. A great, huge satisfying yawn.

'*That's* what yawning is!' I hissed in amazement.

'Not all the time. Sometimes people just yawn. But it *is* the reason people think yawning is contagious.' Mrs Benjamin said. 'It's just a ghost wandering about the room from person to person.'

This made a lot of sense to me.

'So, what *are* you doing here?' I asked. 'Are you ... *stuck*?'

'I think this is just what happens once you pop your clogs.' She sighed, before adding darkly, 'That is unless you somehow get caught up in the strange goings on that have been plaguing the spirit community lately. It's why the others stay inside at night.'

I felt a twitch pincer its way up my spine.

'The *others*?' I asked.

Mrs Benjamin led me down the garden path and together, we peered over her back fence into the park.

For a moment, all I could see was the untidy grass rustling in the night breeze. But then I caught sight of the swing set, which was creaking gently to and fro. Reaching almost instinctively for the wavelength knob, I sharpened it a little.

A small glowing shape was sitting on the swing, its legs dangling. It was counting.

'109, 110, 111, 112, 113 ...'

'Clifford!' Mrs Benjamin called. 'Psst. Clifford! Yoo-hoo!'

The shape looked up and my heart thumped.

It was a boy with his hands over his eyes as if he was playing hide and seek. He was wearing a woolly jumper, a tie and shorts.

'What are you doing outside, Mrs Benjamin!' Clifford hissed as he leapt off the swing and hurried towards us. 'Shouldn't you be hiding by now?'

His hands were still over his eyes as he approached, as if he were frozen permanently like that. When he reached the fence, his fingers separated a little so he could peek at me.

'I *know* that young lady!' he whispered to Mrs Benjamin. 'She sits in that treehouse picking her nose sometimes and then looks at it on the end of her finger.'

'I do *not*!' I cried out, mortified that I'd been caught in that most private of acts.

Clifford nearly toppled over.

'Y-you can *hear* us?!'

'AND see you.' I pointed out, pushing the spectacles up my nose. 'But what's this about hiding? What happens at night?'

'I don't think you need to know about that, Billy.' Mrs Benjamin swept in protectively.

'I can handle it.' I assured her, although deep down I didn't know if I could.

Clifford turned to me. 'It's when the man with the machine with the nozzle comes,' he said darkly, only his eyes visible as he peeped between his fingers. 'We call him ... Dr Dust.'

CHAPTER 5

DR DUST

'He's been hunting ghosts down, sucking us up and carrying us off.' Clifford explained with a grizzly wince.

'Into a machine?!' I asked and Mrs Benjamin nodded. 'B-but where does he take them?'

'No one knows,' Clifford shrugged. 'Ghosts can't leave the place they died. But somehow, he finds them whilst they're sleeping, and once he's sucked them up, he drives off into the night. As if he's *collecting* them.'

I shuddered.

'A few weeks back it was Reggie Porter,' Clifford went on. 'The P.E. teacher from number 12. Lovely fellow. He died almost thirty years ago. Rather an unfortunate incident involving a javelin that ricocheted off a poorly placed garden gnome in his backyard. We all saw Dr Dust coming and hid. But poor Reggie was out in the back garden pole vaulting over the washing line. Then the mist came. And before we knew it, he was drifting over the rooftops and got hoovered up like a ball of fluff up a vacuum—'

'Alright, that's quite enough, Clifford.' Mrs Benjamin warned.

'But don't you see?!' Clifford gasped.
'From what we know Dr Dust isn't *dead*.
He's alive ... and *she's* alive, which means
she can touch anything or go anywhere she
likes. AND most importantly, she can see
ghosts, which means ... she could *help us*!'

My eyes flitted between them.

'NO,' Mrs Benjamin said firmly. 'Billy has
far more to lose than we do, Clifford. And
if you ask me, this Dr Dust character would
be just as dangerous whether you're dead
or not.'

'But surely the others will–'

'NO,' Mrs Benjamin said firmly.

But something else had made the air halt
in the top of my throat, because at that
precise moment there was a huff of irritation
across the park.

'What are you chinwagging about, you nitwits? It's hiding time! Everyone should be tucked in for the night! Clifford, did you count to two hundred? Why aren't you in your letterbox?!'

A surprisingly fleshy-looking ghost leaned over the fence a few doors down. My heart nearly shot out of my chest. His cheeks were puffed, his eyes bulging, and wrapped around his middle was a marching band tuba.

Just like that, peering from behind bushes, peeking over fences and looming behind chimney pots a peppering of ghosts emerged from where they'd been hiding. Glimmers of ribs, spines, gaunt faces and bony fingers. A chimney sweep kid. A lady with hair curlers that were ever so slightly smoking. A flattened cat which slid over the grass like a sting ray, its eyes facing upwards. All sorts of ghosts.

'There's a few of us,' Mrs Benjamin admitted.

'But it won't be that way for long,' Clifford reminded her, then turned to me pleadingly. 'He's trying to catch us all, Billy. We need your help. To find out who he is and why he's doing it, so that we can stop him.'

At that moment, it seemed every ghost in the park had their hollow, faintly glowing eyes fixed on me. Including a tall gaunt lady nearby wearing a long flowing gown who didn't seem to have any eyes, just two dark whirlpools. And with a stab of terror, it all became too much.

'NO!' I shouted, ripping off the spectacles.

As I did so, all of them vanished. And I could hear nothing. Just the faint hum from the streetlights. Relief flooded over me.

But when I felt a yawn coming on and realised that this was most likely a ghost right beside me, I bolted. Fast as I could, pelting for Mrs Benjamin's front gate. I tumbled over her tulips, brushed past her begonias and shimmied my way into our house, up the stairs and under my duvet, as fast as I could.

I felt around for my satin sleep cap between the sheets, and hauled it all the way over my head so it was covering my eyes.

It couldn't be real. It was too much. Too frightening. I didn't owe those ghosts a thing.

But at that moment, in the stuffy heat

beneath by duvet, I felt a faint fluttering breeze on the end of my nose.

My fingers trembling, I peeled back my sleep cap, picked up the spectacles and peered through the lenses with one eye.

There was Hepzibah. Circling around in front of me.

It's a whole different world, I thought as I watched her. The terror and excitement of it all filling my veins in equal measure. *A whole world sitting right in front of me filled with strange spectral folk who NO ONE else knows exist.*

My heart began to thump as what Dev had said earlier about how selfish I could be weasled back into my head.

Excitement battled with terror, as I rustled up an old school notepad, ripped out the used pages and snatched up a nice green pen.

It would be frightening. I was sure of it.

My legs shaking, I went back downstairs making sure not to wake anyone.

You're going to do this, I told myself as I crept along Mrs Benjamin's garden path, any certainty I'd felt just seconds before seeming to become a little floppy for a moment. *You're going to stop Dr Dust.*

I paused beside Mrs Benjamin's lilies and listened. There was absolute silence except for crickets, a distant dog barking. Just a normal night.

But I knew that the second I put the spectacles on, my nights wouldn't ever be normal again.

My neck prickled with excitement.

Unfolding the spectacles, I lowered them to my nose.

My stomach did a roly-poly.

A sea of ghosts, some floating against the sky, the rest of them crowding towards Mrs Benjamin's back fence, stared pleadingly at me.

'Billy?' Mrs Benjamin asked sweetly, folding her hands. 'Are you alright?'

'I *want* to help you,' I told her and then turned to the other ghosts. 'All of you.'

There was a babbled series of 'cheers', 'hurrahs' and thumbs ups from the ghosts without mouths.

'Are you *sure*, Billy?' Mrs Benjamin asked. I could tell she was trying to protect me, but I knew that she must be scared as well, about what would happen if she got sucked up.

'Dying's bad enough without having to be hoovered up,' I told her, taking out my notepad. 'Now, tell me what you know.'

'Billy?'

Mum's voice had come from behind me.

Yanking off the spectacles, I tucked them away.

Mum was in her bathrobe leaning over the fence to our house.

'Billy. It's almost midnight. *What* are you *doing*!'

'Errrrr ...'

Think of something. Think of something.

'Paying ... my respects?' I told her. 'To Mrs Benjamin.'

'Oh,' Mum said, sounding surprised. 'Didn't you call her a mad-crack-old-spoon-collecting-bat just the other week?'

I wanted to roll up like a woodlouse, knowing Mrs Benjamin was in fact stood right beside me.

'That doesn't sound like me.' I lied.

'Yeah, it was after she told you off.' Mum helpfully reminded me. 'Because of the lilies?'

I swiftly changed the subject.

'I just remember how she used to let me decorate her tree every Christmas,' I said to the empty patch of air where Mrs Benjamin had been stood. 'That was fun.'

'Well,' Mum smiled, reaching out to tuck a loose curl of hair under my sleep cap, 'maybe that's enough respect paying for one night. We'll do something nice to remember her tomorrow. Come on. Bed.'

After Mum tucked me in and quizzed me a few times to make sure everything really was alright, I lay awake gazing at the ceiling.

Over at my bedroom window there was
a rattling as if the glass was shaking. And
sitting up, I wedged my spectacles on.

Clifford, his hands still on his face, was
pressed up against my bedroom window,
peering through his fingers and blowing with
all his might.

'How come you can be up here?' I hissed as I opened the window. 'I thought ghosts were stuck were they died.'

'That's the thing, you see.' Clifford lowered himself to my windowsill. 'Did you ever hear that there used to be a Ferris Wheel in Stony Brook?'

I knew the story well. I could even remember Ma telling me the headline:

STONY BROOK BOY, 12, CATAPAULTED FROM RUNAWAY FERRIS WHEEL

'That was YOU?' I gaped. 'But that happened when my mums were little.'

'I remember covering my eyes as I was flying up high above the town. And then I must have died of terror somewhere up there in the sky. I think that because I was mid-air when I passed away, I couldn't be anchored to the spot where I died. I can move around anywhere outside. But not inside.'

'So you can't come into my room?' I asked.

'Not across any indoor threshold, I'm afraid.' Clifford explained, tapping his foot on what seemed like invisible glass in the frame of my window.

I reached for my notebook.

'So, Dr Dust,' I redirected Clifford's focus. 'What other clues have you got? What does he look like?'

Clifford crossed his legs on the windowsill.

'He wears a white sort of hazmat suit with a hood,' he said, darkly. 'A mask, a respirator mask with two snouts. And he drives this contraption down the streets releasing a mist that seems to completely immobilise ghosts. Once they're floating in a trance, he sucks them up using a pipe on the back of his machine. And then off he goes.'

'What about his face?' I asked, writing it all down. 'Any notable features? A nice thick moustache? A tattoo? A scar in the shape of a bone?'

'I couldn't say for certain,' Clifford said. 'When we see the mist coming from over the rooftops, everyone hides indoors. Except me. I usually use the letter box or if there's a parcel inside it, the rubbish bin. Somewhere he can't find me.'

'Wouldn't the parcel just ... sit inside you?' I asked, curious about ghost physics.

'Well, it could, but it's awfully uncomfortable.' Clifford explained. 'Gives one the hiccups.'

Poor Clifford. I thought. Though I realised he must be the one who blew our post all over the footpath and the reason why my subscription to *Kids in the Park Magazine* always got wet.

'You can't think of anything else?' I asked. 'Nothing specific?'

Clifford looked pensive.

'There is *one* thing. It's probably not important. But on the back of his machine, it says "Dr Dust" in silver letters. That's why we call him that.'

'Dr *Dust*,' I puzzled. 'Do you think that's his *real* name?'

Clifford shrugged as Hepzibah swam out from the pile of laundry at the bottom of my bed and did a little loop around him.

'Right,' I finished off my notes. 'I'll knuckle down into this investigating tomorrow.'

I felt quite excited at the prospect. If only Dev was talking to me, we could have started a sort of committee or an agency and split the work in half. Shared it. Dev and I used to share everything. Not just blueberry muffins.

'One last thing,' I said to Clifford, putting away my pen. 'There aren't any ...' I dropped to a very low whisper. 'Any ... *ghosts* who live in my house ... are there?'

'There used to be,' Clifford said mysteriously, slowly floating away a little from my windowsill. 'A woman with a very tall hat that lived in your attic. And she used to scream like an alarm clock all night. Something about a missing suitcase.'

'Wh-what happened to her?' I asked, wondering if this were the reason why Ma always complained that the attic windows rattled.

'Slllurpck!' Clifford said grimly, as if sucking a straw. 'Hoovered up.'

Jude started crying and I heard Mums' bedroom door open.

'I'll come find you tomorrow,' I told Clifford. 'Make sure you find somewhere safe to sleep tonight!'

Clifford winked between his fingers and dived off my windowsill. I saw him drifting down over Ma's workshop before vanishing into the woodpile at the back.

I slid the spectacles off my face, folded them beside my bed and rubbed my nose.

My head was thrumming as thoughts

bounced back and forth off the walls of my brain like an endless screensaver.

There was a faint tickle on the end of my nose.

'Night, Hepzibah,' I whispered.

It was going to be a tricky old mission.

Finding this Dr Dust. But find him I would.

And stop him.

Because no one was going to get their hands on my dead goldfish.

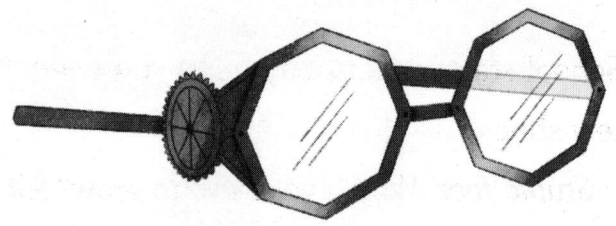

CHAPTER 6

BERNARD SOLOMON'S SPECIALIST SPECTACLES

'Can't we go another day?' I moaned, trying to do my pleading face.

Looking cute used to work on Mum. And then suddenly one day, the exact day Jude was born in fact, it was like she stopped finding me cute anymore.

'No. Today's the only day your aunt's free to take you.' Mum said flatly, wrestling Jude into a bib as he tried to chew her hair.

'School starts in four days, and you need new shoes.'

Stupid feet. Why'd you have to grow? All I could think about was getting on with my investigation. I'd even set myself up at the desk in my room with Mum's iPad like I was at a real office when she rudely interrupted.

Aunty Coral is only ten years older than I am. Which makes me feel like I don't have to listen to what she says as much. She's not that bad really. We've actually had some nice times together, but there's just these things she says that drive me up the wall.

'Billy-Booby-Boo!'

That.

Aunty Coral gave me a hug that felt like she was trying to pull my head off my shoulders. 'Shoe-shopping, girl, you ready?'

I tried to squeeze out a smile.

'One for the Gram, Billy-Babes?' She squidged her face up against mine and took a photo without my permission.

'And … posted!' she laughed, sounding like a parrot that's hit a windshield. 'Now. Do you need a special car seat or anything?'

'I'm nine *years* old.' I reminded her. 'Not nine *months*.'

To add insult to injury, she made me sit in the back seat. She said it was because there was too much stuff on the front seat, but I knew the truth.

Garbles Discount Shoe Warehouse was in the middle of town in the arcade, just down the road from the Mums' antique shop.

'So many shops closing, huh?' Aunty Coral said as we drove past empty shop fronts. Whenever she turned a corner, the pile of phone chargers, a hairdryer and an empty box of tissues on the front seat lurched about.

'They're trying to build a shopping centre,' I told her bitterly, feeling the pocket of my dungarees to make sure the spectacles were still there. I didn't want to risk leaving them at home.

'Ohhh, that would be nice.'

I was going to tell her no; it wouldn't be nice AT ALL because it meant that little shops like Mums' one would be knocked down to a powdery crumble. But I couldn't be bothered wasting my breath.

'Doesn't look like there are any parking spaces,' Aunty Coral said. 'I'll channel some positive vibes.'

She reached out with her clacky little nails and held the purple crystal hanging from her rear-view mirror.

Pfft. I thought, *as if that's going to wo–*

'Yay! Look a spot!' Aunty Coral squealed, reversing her little bubble-gum pink Mini.

As we walked into Garbles, Aunty Coral was distracted by someone commenting on the picture she'd posted. And from the corner of my eye, I noticed a tiny shop tucked into the passage of the arcade.

I was pretty sure I'd never seen it before.

It was very narrow. With a flaking silver sign, its windows crammed with eye charts, lenses and twists of wire.

BERNARD SOLOMON'S SPECIALIST SPECTACLES

Come in today for a free eye test!

That's it! I realised. *The shop where the spectacles were made.*

The shoe warehouse was chaos. Mums bashed past with boys in tow, hunting for rugby boots. Kids tore tissue paper as they searched for another size six. We chose a pair of shoes that Aunty Coral said were 'the least hideous ones available' and burst out of Garbles gasping for air.

'I was thinking we could go get our nails done!' said Aunty Coral. 'Girls day, yay!'

I needed to nip that misconception right in the bud.

'Err ... actually ... I know something better,' I swallowed. 'I did it once and it's *REALLY* fun.'

'Ooooh! Whatcha thinking?'

'We could both ...' I did a fake drumroll. 'Get an eye test!'

I waved my hands in the direction of the Specialist Spectacles shop.

'Oh,' Aunty Coral said, sounding disappointed. 'Are you sure you don't want–'

'Yep!' I said brightly.

* * *

A bell rang as we entered the dim shop, a greenish fluorescent light blinking.

'Hello?' Aunty Coral called out.

I could see from the way she clutched her

handbag that she did *not* like being there.

The most unusual glasses were propped on little displays all over the shop. Some looked as if they were made from bone and shaped like crescent moons. Others were wooden and lumpy and there even a few that were rusty with big rivets around the eyepieces.

'Here to collect?' came a crackly little voice from beyond the dusty velvet curtain behind the counter.

'Err ...' I swallowed. 'We're after eye-tests?'

'Ah!' The curtain parted and a very small man, whose head was completely bald save for a tired looking sprig of white hair protruding from his forehead.

He doddered around the counter.

'One at a time.' He gestured at my aunt to sit in the squeaky-looking little chair at the front of the shop.

Aunty Coral took out a make-up wipe and gave the chair a quick clean before sitting carefully down.

'Stool?' the old gentleman said to me.

'I beg your pardon?'

'Would you please sit on the stool.' He repeated pointing to a green stool behind the counter.

I followed instructions, watching carefully as he swung what looked like a pair of science-fiction binoculars on an extendable arm in front of me.

'A-are you *Bernard Solomon*?' I asked. 'Like the name of the shop?'

'I am,' he said, straining to adjust the

knobs and lenses on the enormous eye-testing machine. 'Look straight ahead for me.'

Mr. Solomon slotted a slide into the machine, flicked on a light and I peered inside. Rows of letters in descending sizes appeared before me.

'Do-do you make *all* the glasses in your shop?' I asked.

'I do indeed,' Mr. Solomon said, adjusting the rings around the eyepieces. 'Can you read the bottom line for me and tell me if it's crystal clear, readable or fuzzy?'

'A-P-X-B-Z-L-E-N,' I read aloud. 'Crystal clear. And do any of them ... do anything special?'

'What sort of special?' he croaked, changing the slide again and flicking some lenses in and out so the letters blurred for a moment.

'Well ...' I began. 'Do any of them make you ... see things ... things that aren't really there?'

For a moment, just a tiny moment, the old man stopped, his raisin-like eyes wincing.

'What sorts of things?'

I swallowed. Certain he was going to let out a great roar of laughter.

'Um ... rgh ... ghosts?' I whispered.

'I see,' Mr. Solomon said, glancing over at Aunty Coral, as if to check if she was listening. 'Well ... I suppose none of us *truly* knows what might lurk in dimensions beyond our own. But then again, there is every chance it is only a smudge on the lens or crack in a mirror that makes us think we've seen a ghost. Now ...' he changed his tone. 'Back in a tick. Just going to fetch a slide from the back.'

Mr. Solomon bumbled into the back of his shop, disappearing from view for a moment.

I sighed. It seemed like this was a dead end. Mrs Benjamin definitely wasn't a smudge. And Clifford wasn't a crack. Maybe the Spectracles had just been put in a mismatched case and Mr. Solomon didn't make them at all?

'Ah yes,' Mr. Solomon coughed, re-emerging as he clutched a slide which he slotted in front of the eyepieces. 'Knew I had it somewhere. Could you read this one for me, but only the first letter of each word.'

'D-N-R,' I began, but only when I'd started did I clock what the slide really said:

DO NOT REACT TO THIS MESSAGE.
KEEP READING AS REQUESTED.
THE SPECTACLES IN YOUR
POSSESSION ARE ENORMOUSLY
RARE AND OF GREAT VALUE.
I MADE THEM TO ORDER FOR
A DANGEROUS PERSON WHO
THREATENED ME. AND I WANT
NOTHING MORE TO DO WITH THEM.

GET RID OF THEM AS FAST AS
YOU CAN. OR DESTROY THEM.
TELL NO ONE.

AND NEVER COME HERE AGAIN!

Dangerous person?

That had to be Dr Dust. And it made feel sick to the stomach.

I was bursting with hundreds of questions but didn't dare so much as open my mouth.

'Right!' Mr. Solomon snapped, yanking the slide out and prodding me off the stool. 'That's all we've got time for. I have to close shop.'

'Well, what about *my* eye test?' Aunty Coral frowned.

'Your eyes look just fine to me,' he said, ushering us towards the door.

I knew this wasn't true because no one that wears a t-shirt with 'Freaking Fabulous!' written in tiny crystals on it can have perfect eyesight.

'That's it. Out. Out you go!' Mr. Solomon waved us back into the arcade. 'Good day!'

As soon as we were out the door, Mr. Solomon bolted it and flicked the sign to 'CLOSED.' The lights switched off, and he vanished into the back of his dusty establishment.

'Bit of an oddball.' Aunty Coral said.

Takes one to know one, I thought.

CHAPTER 7

BACK TO SCHOOL

That weekend before school started back, I managed to do two things. Firstly, I found an old birdhouse in Ma's workshop that she no longer wanted. I dusted it down, painted it duck-egg blue and hung it on the crab-apple tree outside my window. Secondly, I managed to wangle an extra half-hour of iPad time by loading the dishwasher on Saturday night.

Gathering all the intel that the ghosts had given me I tried to Google for clues.

HAZMAT SUIT

RESPIRATOR MASK

MACHINE WITH NOZZLE (VACUUM CLEANER MAYBE?)

DR DUST

But the only things I could find on the internet were industrial street cleaners. And whenever I typed in 'Dr Dust', it kept coming up with some time of special air filter for old people that got rid of dust mites.

I needed something more concrete to go on. There had to be other ghosts out there who had seen this 'Dr Dust' and had a better idea of what was happening.

On Sunday night, Ma washed my hair, and Mum made me lay out all my clothes ready for school the next morning. With Dev still not talking to me, I didn't feel excited about Year Five at all. And I felt even less excited about it when I overheard a conversation Mums were having in the kitchen.

'Maybe we *should* sell.' Mum murmured to Ma 'It's not like the shop's making any money. And on the rare occasion we sell something it's just enough to cut even. What do you think?'

Ma sighed and gave Mum a tight hug. A sad hug.

I didn't want them to sell *Past Life*. That was their special project. They'd met at an antiques fair. It was part of their story.

I tried to distract myself by searching furiously for clues on the iPad, but a rattling at my window disturbed me.

Taking the spectacles from where I'd hidden them in the box my new school shoes came in, I slipped them on.

'Dr Dust struck again!' Clifford told me like an old-timey newspaper seller pressed up against my window.

'Who was it this time?' I asked.

'Saul Grouse, the tuba player, from number thirty-six.'

I remembered him. He was the one who was reminding the others to hide.

'He was in the front garden, practising a

lively march.' Clifford panted. 'We tried to warn him to find somewhere safe to hide, but he mustn't have heard us. Before we knew it there was one loud B-flat *parp*! and he was sucked away.'

My spine twitched at the thought, but I noted everything down.

'I've got school tomorrow. But I'm going to speak to other ghosts if I can.' I told Clifford. 'See if Dr Dust is hunting all over town or just on this street.'

Clifford nodded.

'Oh, and I found you somewhere to sleep. Somewhere of your own.' I pointed over to the little birdhouse I'd hung from the tree.

'Super!' Clifford dove off the sill and straight into the birdhouse.

There was a small *burst* of feathers, and

with a startled squawk a panicked-looking blackbird shot out from the opening. Through the birdhouse's window there was a faint glow as Clifford cosied up for the night.

* * *

This was the first year I was allowed to walk to school on my own which was a lot more fun than I thought it would be. The leaves were just beginning to turn roasted brown and crunchy under foot. And my heart felt strangely light as I marched to school, an investigation underway and the proud new owner of a highly sought after and mysterious set of spectacles. I was like Miss Marple, only less ancient. But I didn't feel quite as cool when I spotted Dev with some new friends on the edge of the school garden patch.

He had a round tin with him and was handing out something he'd baked. Judging from the jealous whiff that caught my nostrils across the playground, it was his legendary cinnamon and apple buns.

It seemed that since he dumped me on my lonesome all the other kids in our year had finally realised how awesome he really was.

That was the problem with having one best friend. When they're gone it's just you.

When break swung by, I found myself alone on the steps leading up to the music rooms chewing on one of Mum's peanut butter and plantain chip 'don't knock it till you've tried it' sandwiches.

Who cares about Dev! I tried to tell

myself. *I've got hundreds of new friends now. Sure, no-one except me can see them. And one of them's a ninety-two-year-old lady. But so what?*

I had my investigation to get on with.

Stuffing my sandwich wrapper into my pocket I felt around for my spectacles, wondering which part of the school would be the quietest for me to start ghost hunting.

'Hiya, Billy. You on your own too, eh?' came a deep voice from just nearby.

Dorothy Mooney, or Dorothy 'Moo' as she was known had somehow materialised beside me.

She was called that because she was very tall with knobbly knees. EXCEPTIONALLY tall I'd say. The sort of tall you notice first in class photos. She had two long plaits that somehow made her look even taller and mournful eyes with long eyelashes that wouldn't be out of place chewing grass in a meadow.

I don't approve of everyone going on about how tall she is all the time. Ma and Mum said that when they first had me as a baby, people kept pointing out the fact that I was going to have two mums. They said that if you notice something different about someone there is absolutely NO NEED to mention it, even if you're trying to be nice, or even if you desperately want to. Those people are most probably reminded every single day that they're different so there's no call whatsoever to draw their attention to it.

Which is why I felt sorry for Dorothy Moo.

'Yep. All alone,' I smiled at Dorothy, planning very much to keep it that way.

'Oh gosh.' Dorothy said slowly. 'That's no good, is it?'

'Works for me,' I lied, glancing over at Dev who was laughing his socks off as Maeve Binks told him what was apparently an incredibly funny joke. You would find that impossible to believe if you'd ever met Maeve 'I've-Already-Finished-Miss!' Binks.

I tried to slink away towards the school hall, which looked like the oldest building at our school and was hopefully swimming with ghosts, but when I glanced over my shoulder, Dorothy was trotting after me.

Rats.

I did a loop once around the toilet block and then made a mad dash behind the gym, eventually losing her to a throng of girls using a skipping rope.

I checked the coast was clear and slipped through the double doors. The hall was empty, lined with rows of stackable chairs.

With my notepad and pen handy, I pulled out my spectacles from my backpack and wedged them on.

There were two large curtains to either side of the stage, and unless I was much mistaken, one of them seemed to be dancing a little in the wind.

I approached it cautiously, taking the side steps.

Sure enough, from behind it, I heard voices. And music. Terrible, scribbly music.

'You've got fingers like unripe bananas, Sister Mary-Martin!' The voice was spiky, and sharp.

'Hello?' I whispered.

'Come on, sister!' The voice rallied. 'Light a fire underneath that bottom of yours.

You're stiff as a wooden board, girl! Play it like you mean it! Give it what for!'

I reached out and peeled back the velvet curtain.

Two nuns in long black habits appeared. One was wiry with a pinched face and stood beside the grand piano on the school stage. The other had dimples, one little curl of hair poking out of her wimple and was blowing violently into a flute.

Our school used to be a convent, so I wasn't overly surprised at the ghosts' appearance.

'H-hello there,' I began. Both of them turned. The one beside the piano fixed her beetle black eyes on me. With a shriek, she flew across the stage her wimple flaring out behind her as she blew with all her might.

What she was hoping to do I didn't know. Because all I felt was a tiny flutter of air on my eyelid.

I held my ground.

'If it isn't another unteachable child!' she wailed. 'Hammering away at this poor old girl's ivories like she's an old tavern honky-tonk!'

'Actually, I don't play the piano. Tried the clarinet once. Hated it,' I said. Her pinched face tightened in shock.

'Sister Mary-John ...' the flute nun gasped in a whisper. 'I think she can *see* us!'

'Nonsense, Sister Mary-Martin.' Sister Mary-John huffed, and reaching out, she waved her ruler through my stomach.

I yawned.

'No *wonder* everyone's always so sleepy in assembly,' I realised. 'Must be you two waltzing about in here.'

'What devilish implement allows you to see us, child?' Sister Mary-John barked.

'Look,' I told them both pragmatically. 'I don't want to take up much of your precious time, but I've been speaking to other people in your ... your ... *community*. And there's been talk of a man at night sucking up ghosts using a machine. I wondered if you'd heard or seen anything?'

The two nuns gaped at one another.

'Why … that's precisely what happened to our Mother Superior. Sister Mary-Cecilia.'

'Oh?' I asked.

'We had a trio,' Sister Mary-Martin told me. 'The Holy Spirits we were called. We used to play for the other ghosts at the school.'

I began to take notes.

'But one day,' Sister Mary-Martin went on with a ghostly tear in her pale eyes, 'we were rehearsing on the hockey field. Sister Mary-Cecilia was half-way through her solo on the tenor saxophone, when a strange mist appeared. That's when we saw him. Pushing his strange machine. Sister Mary-Cecilia was lifted up, still laying down some sweet tunes like the red-hot jumpin' jazz cat she was. And the last thing we heard was ...' She paused to wipe a tear with the sleeve of her habit. *'Beep. Beep. Extractor reversing.'*

'Beep, beep extractor reversing?' I repeated softly, writing this down. 'What do you think that was?'

'Heavens knows.' Sister Mary-Martin sighed heavily, making a note come out of her flute as she did so.

At that moment the bell rang.

'I need to get to class,' I told the sisters. 'But if you think of anything else, please come find me. Make me yawn twice so I'll know it's you.'

I slipped off my spectacles, pulled back the curtain and froze. Dorothy Mooney was sat in the school hall. Watching me with her hands folded.

'Nice specs,' she said.

'I was ...' I blurted out. 'Practicing lines ... for ... err ... a *school play* ... yes ... that's it, a school play.'

I hurried down the aisle between the chairs, towards the double doors.

'Well ...' Dorothy clopped after me as I ducked between the other kids scurrying back to class, 'It did sound an awful lot, like you *were* talking to someone. Someone who wasn't really there, if you know what I mean.'

'No,' I insisted. 'I don't know what you mean.'

'My dad has a ghost,' Dorothy announced loudly.

I stopped dead in my tracks.

CHAPTER 8

PET FEARS

I pulled Dorothy aside by the crook of her elbow so no one could hear us.

'What do you mean your dad "has a ghost"?' I asked.

'Well …' Dorothy shook her heads slightly. 'He *had* a ghost. It's someone else's ghost now, I suppose.'

'What are you *on* about?' I hissed.

I wanted to turn her upside down like a saltshaker and joggle it out of her.

'He *had* a pet shop.' Dorothy told me. 'He sold it just the other day. *Feline Lucky.*'

Feline Lucky was where we'd bought Hepzibah. It was just a couple of shops down from Mums' shop.

'There was a ghost?' I asked.

Most of the other kids had vanished into classrooms. I needed to be quick.

'Yes. That's why he had to sell the shop.'

'Billy Duggery!'

I glanced over at Mr Mensah who was tapping his watch warningly.

'Meet me at the gates after school,' I told Dorothy. 'You need to tell me *everything.*'

* * *

'It started with small things,' Dorothy explained as we walked into Stony Brook together after school. 'One day the ball python somehow escaped and cornered a little girl. Dad got a lot of bad reviews for that. Then the next week, the guinea pigs chewed through their cage and shot off into Stony Brook Woods, where they're still terrorising any walkers carrying snacks. Then there was the incident involving Evangeline, our tarantula.'

Dorothy swallowed.

'She's usually very friendly, but something must have spooked her, because when Dad was cleaning out her tank, she reared up and jumped right onto a sphynx cat this lady was buying. The cat freaked out and scratched the lady. The lady then freaked out, screamed and fell backwards into the octopus aquarium. And the octopus went wild, pulling things off the shelves until it galumphed into the back of the shop and vanished down the toilet.'

I made notes of everything Dorothy was saying.

'Cat … octopus … toilet …'

'After that, customers stopped coming,' Dorothy said sadly. 'He had no choice but to sell it to Bullham's Developments.'

Those were the people who wanted to buy Mums' shop.

'You know me, Billy,' Dorothy went, 'I'll always look for the most practical explanation.'

I didn't want to be impolite, but the truth was I didn't know Dorothy that well at all. But I had heard that she was something of a mad scientist and won all sorts of glamorous prizes for it.

Dorothy went on. 'But the only clue that anything strange had happened was a peculiar reading in the electromagnetic field around the shop.'

We stopped outside *Feline Lucky* which was boarded up. The shop had a black and white striped door with pale pink and green rims around the windows. And plastered across its glass window was a large 'SOLD' sign.

'There's a back door that doesn't lock properly,' Dorothy said.

We snuck into the alley behind the shop. Dorothy fished out a sheet of paper from her backpack and folded it into a triangle.

Slotting it into the gap between the door frame and the lock, she wiggled it around.

There was a *click* as the latch sprung loose.

I turned to Dorothy.

'Before we do this. You have to swear. Absolutely swear. Swear on … on …'

I tried to think of something she loved.

'On *science* that you won't tell anybody. Not a single soul about *anything* we're talking about. OK?'

'Whatever you say, Billy,' Dorothy smiled amenably.

I reached for the spectacles in my pocket. As the door closed behind us, the shop was silent. Nothing but clumps of fur and a bag of hamster pellets spilling onto the floor. As if something had clawed its way into it.

Taking a deep breath, I lowered the spectacles to my nose.

Nothing.

Was Dorothy Mooney having me on?

'I can't see anything,' I whispered, twisting the wavelength knobs. 'Are you sure—'

There was a hideous bellow. I stumbled backwards.

This ghost wasn't like any of the others I'd seen before. It was wild. And terrifying. Blurry and flickering.

The ghost's eyes glowed a pale soulless green. And as its mouth snared open, I saw its teeth were long and twisted.

'WHEEEEEERRRREE AMMMMMM IIIIIIIIIIII!????' it screeched.

'I'm Billy …' I stammered. 'I'm trying to—' Dorothy walked into the shop ahead of me. I panicked and tried to stop her. But completely forgot that she could neither hear nor see the ghost.

'WHHHHAAAAAT AM I DOOOOOOOING HERRRRRRRE?!'

The ghost was wearing gym shorts and shouting into a megaphone. A javelin poked out of its back.

It's the P.E. teacher, I thought. *The one who vanished from number 12.*

Clifford had said he was lovely.

This *couldn't* be the same ghost.

'GETTTTTTT OOOOOOOUUUUUT!' the ghost roared, and I very nearly did. Thankfully, I had the presence of mind to remember his name.

'REGGIE!' I shouted. 'We just want to help you!'

'Who's Reggie?' Dorothy asked, completely unaware that she'd just walked right through him. 'Nice specs, by the way, Billy. Are they prescription?'

I tried to focus.

'NOOOOONNE CAN HELP ME!' The ghost screamed, clawing at the walls with his long fingers. 'GEETTTTTTTT OUUUUUUUUT!'

Using the javelin in his back like a pole vault, he sprung towards me. I charged out of the shop and Dorothy calmly followed.

'So?' Dorothy asked.

'There's a ghost alright,' I trembled. 'He was from my street. He was ghostnapped. But I don't understand why he's *here*.'

I chewed on my thoughts and then turned to Dorothy.

'Do you *really* promise not to tell anyone?' I asked her anxiously.

'Scouts honour,' Dorothy saluted.

'These,' I handed Dorothy the spectacles, 'are not normal spectacles. You can see ghosts through them.'

Dorothy lowered them to her nose and peered studiously through the small back window into the shop.

I held my breath, thinking she was going to shriek with fright and shoot off down the alley. But instead ...

'Oh, yes,' she said flatly. 'Extraordinary. Quite explains the unusual spikes in electromagnetic readings I took.'

She handed me back the spectacles.

'But aren't you shocked?' I asked.

'Not really. Paranormal Exposition is a

little side hobby of mine,' Dorothy explained. 'There's far too many instances of people seeing things for it to all be *complete* nonsense, so I try to bring a more scientific approach to the subject.'

As we walked back home, I told Dorothy everything. About the man in the beanie who had buried the spectacles outside the antique shop. About Clifford, Mrs Benjamin, Hepzibah and the strange stories of Dr Dust.

'Why do you think the man in the beanie was trying to get rid of the spectacles?' Dorothy asked.

I realised I hadn't thought about it.

'He seemed ... scared,' I told her, thinking back. 'It was as if ... he was worried there was someone watching him.'

My mind began to thrum.

'Maybe someone was threatening him?' I suggested, remembering what Mr Solomon had said.

'Perhaps,' Dorothy murmured.

We stopped for a single scoop each at *We All Scream*, the Stony Brook ice-cream shop. Dorothy very obligingly got the bill.

'Can you see *everyone* who's died through the spectacles?' she asked.

'I think so,' I nodded, devouring my white chocolate and blackberry in a cone.

'In that case, I know someone who might be able to help us,' she said. 'Someone who used to specialise in studying the paranormal, and then passed on to ... the other side. I'll introduce you this weekend.'

CHAPTER 9

SWAMPBOTTOM LAKE

On Friday night, Mum came home from work looking a little shaken.

'Have a nice cup of ginger lemon tea.' Aunty Coral said pushing it into her hand. She was baby-sitting Jude that day.

'I can't believe it,' Mum stuttered.

'Tell us!' Aunty Coral encouraged, nestling down opposite her, ready to hear the gossip.

I listened from the kitchen table where I was pretending to finish homework. 'I sold this

lady an antique gramophone a few weeks ago,'
Mum explained in a low voice. I don't think
she wanted me to hear. 'She was a cellist and
wanted to play some old cello records she has.
But she came back today insisting I give her
a refund. She said that when she practiced
her cello at night, even when it was switched
off, she could hear a *voice* coming out of the
gramophone, shouting the most torrid abuse.'

I squinted with my ear in Mum's direction.

'A *voice*?' Aunty Coral snorted.

Mum nodded and took a swig.

'She left a horrible review of the shop
online saying that we'd played a prank
on her, and we didn't have a single other
customer for the rest of the day.'

'But what did this voice say?' Aunty
Coral asked.

'Whenever she picked up her cello, it started to scream and wail and said, "*You call that a b-flat, you talentless muppet? I could play a better b-flat with my rear-end!*"'

Aunty Coral looked alarmed.

A thought occurred to me. *Was it the saxophone-playing Mother Superior from school?*

I was starting to see a pattern.

Ghosts were sucked into Dr Dust's machine and then released in another location. But something happened to them in between. Something that made them turn wild ... and ghoulish.

I needed to act. And fast. Before every ghost in town, Hepzibah, Mrs Benjamin and Clifford included, was turned into the raving

monster we'd seen earlier that day and
the whole of Stony Brook descended into
terrifying chaos.

* * *

The next morning, I set out to meet Dorothy.

She was a tiny speck when I saw her down
the road in the distance. She started waving
when she spotted me and didn't stop until I
was just a few steps away.

'Err ... what's that you got there?' I asked.

Dangling over Dorothy's shoulder was a
small radar dish attached to what looked like
some type of converted hairdryer.

'I call it the Ecto-Plasma Wave Subsystem,'
Dorothy explained. 'I've been devising it
for a few years now. It picks up something

I'm temporarily calling "Para-Sonic Sound".
Patent pending.'

'So … you mean, you can *hear* ghosts
using that thing?'

'Not quite,' Dorothy admitted. 'I'm hoping
that the person we're going to see will be
able to help me with the finishing touches.
Scientific exploration of the paranormal runs
in my family.'

As we headed out of town and began to
pick our way along the brook through Hen
Rock Woods, Dorothy explained some more.

'My grandad, on my mother's side, was a
crypto scientist. Professor Sinus Wuft. He
invented a kind of perfume called *Ghost-
Off!*' She pulled out a violet and silver
coffin-shaped bottle from her backpack and
handed it to me.

GHOST-OFF!

Wild Sage and Grave Florals

By Wuft

Keep those dearly departed,
departed for good.

I flipped over the bottle.

For use as a personal scent or as a home fragrance. A gentle spritz of Ghost-Off is guaranteed to keep you and your home phantom-free thanks to its three-tier spirit immobiliser technology. Also available in a range of other scents including 'Cemetery Bouquet', 'Summer Tombstones' and 'Grandma's Soap'.

'Needless to say,' Dorothy said as I handed it back. 'People thought he was completely mad: loads of other scientists called him a scam artist. He became a recluse, but continued to research the paranormal until one of his experiments went wrong and he died in his lab.'

Dorothy led me off the path, fighting her way through the moss and low hanging branches as mosquitoes gnawed at our legs. With a flourish, she pulled aside the branch of a large fern. A rundown house, half of which was sinking into Swampbottom Lake came into view.

We picked our way around the lake towards the sunken house.

The front door was at an angle, and protruding from the muddy ground were an assortment of faded homemade signs:

NO TRESPASSING

MOVE ALONG!

NOTHING TO SEE HERE!!!

RACK OFF!

Dorothy unhooked the hairdryer-ish thing from her belt and, adjusting her radar, pointed it towards the door.

There was a *crackling* followed by what sounded almost exactly like a bagpipe.

'I think he's still here,' Dorothy whispered.

Fumbling around in my backpack, I fished out the spectacles and put them on.

My heart thumping, Dorothy and I slowly approached the door.

Inside, the house had two levels, a crooked staircase in the middle and floorboards that sloped down into the murky water.

'H-hello?' I called, nervously. I had discovered over the last few days that not all ghosts were friendly.

Dorothy's radar machine wailed and crackled.

The floorboards creaked beneath us as we wobbled across, trying not to slide into the water.

'I don't see anything,' I whispered.

'Let's check upstairs.'

At the top of the overgrown staircase, abandoned laboratory apparatuses and mouldy jars filled with strange liquids were stacked all over the place.

At an angle underneath the big round window that looked out over Swampbottom Lake was a desk littered with equipment, a bucket with a mop and a large armchair covered in a stained sheet.

'Nothing.' I muttered. *Maybe Dorothy had got it wrong?*

Dorothy pointed her radar at the armchair. The noise transformed from a waily bagpiping to something more like a snoring trumpet.

My breath caught in my throat.

A pair of shoes poked out from underneath the sheet.

I gave Dorothy a signal, and we crept closer and closer until with a silent, 'One, two, three!' I yanked the sheet away.

And to my horror, sat very still in the armchair, was a pair of very long legs completely separated from any body.

CHAPTER 10

PROFESSOR SINUS WUFT

I let out a shout.

There was a high-pitched grunt from the radar. Followed by a snort.

I swivelled, and what I had previously thought was a manky, old, mop head toppled off the bucket it was perched on and onto the floor.

The object raised itself into the air.

It was a head. A *human* head. Of an old man with a puckered mouth. The head was wearing glasses. Floating all by itself right in front me.

It drew closer, peering at my spectacles.

'That's *Spectre*-Glass!' it rasped, squinting at my spectacles. 'Arms, get yourselves over here!'

From over my shoulder, two willowy arms flew through the air, one clasping a notepad, the other a pencil. They perched themselves in midair next to the legs.

'P-p-professor Sinus Wuft?' I asked.

'Indeed I am,' the head nodded, its long white hair dangling underneath it, thankfully covering up whatever gory remains of a neck there were.

'And the glass in your spectacles, *madam*, is *my* invention! Though how it ended up in a pair of cheap, gag spectacles is quite beyond me!'

'Maybe we should start from the beginning,' I suggested. 'This is your granddaughter, Dorothy ...'

'Granddaughter, you say?' the head said sounding delighted. 'Can she see me too?'

'Here,' I handed Dorothy the spectacles.

'Hello there, Grandad!' Dorothy waved her radar. 'Couldn't help me with this, could you?'

I watched as Dorothy and her invisible grandfather worked.

'Yes, of course. Quite right,' Dorothy said to mid-air. 'That makes sense. I'll just make a small adjustment here and–'

The radar gave a *wibble* and I heard Professor Wuft's glitchy voice emitting from Dorothy's speaker.

'I see uncommon height and good long legs has continued to run in the family then, eh? You know what they say. Taller people = higher thinking.'

Dorothy beamed, holding up her radar gun.

I gave a small cough.

'Oh, sorry, Billy,' Dorothy murmured, and then whispered to mid-air in front of her. 'She's not very sciency, Grandad.'

'Poor thing,' Professor Wuft tutted. 'Rather short, eh? Daft as a brush then, I'll bet?'

'You know I *can* hear you,' I reminded them.

Dorothy smiled apologetically, handing me the spectacles.

'We need your help,' I told the professor. 'Someone is prowling Stony Brook at night, immobilising ghosts with a type of mist. The ghosts call him Dr Dust.'

Professor Wuft's head settled back on top of the legs, his hands sticking out from near his ears.

'An *immobilising* mist, you say?'

'Yes,' I went on. 'And once the ghosts can't move, he sucks them up into a machine.'

Wuft's eyes widened.

'So, it's finally happening then? That ... that ... *wazzock* who stole my research is putting it to use!'

I frowned.

'You mean your perfume?

'Yes,' Wuft lamented. 'There's only one substance on the planet that could so effectively lull ghosts to sleep. And that's *Ghost-Off*. But I invented *Ghost-Off* with the most noble of intentions: to gently introduce people to the invisible wavelength that sits alongside our own. It was *never* intended for this!'

'So then, you think you know what Dr Dust is doing?' I asked.

Wuft grimaced. 'He's *severing* them. Separating them from the place they died. Which is like ... plucking a snail from its shell. A loathsome act with hideous consequences for the poor soul involved.'

I thought about Reggie Porter, the gym teacher with his snaring mouth and drilling eyes.

'No doubt this Dr Dust character is planning something, using my real life's work.'

Dorothy and I glanced at one another.

'Your *real* life's work?' I asked.

The head turned towards us and smiled.

'The Wavelength Portal Refractor 3000.'

'What did it do?' I asked, note-taking furiously.

'It was a transporter.' Wuft's eyes gleamed. 'A conveyer of objects between wavelengths. With a simple push of a button, I was hoping to send things through a Spectre-Glass prism, from our world into the realms beyond. But alas, on the day I was due to reveal the machine to the press, I discovered that the Spectre-Glass had been stolen.'

'Stolen?' I repeated.

'Yes. Without it, the machine couldn't work. I was made a laughingstock by newspapers across the country, withdrew from the public eye. And shortly afterwards had my little … well, accident. A distractingly delicious sandwich, a wrong measurement, a vial of rubidium and one hearty explosion later my body was …. rearranged, as you see.'

The enormously long legs crossed themselves.

'I was now a ghost, confined to this laboratory; marooned in the spectral wavelength. And had to watch helplessly as people in dark coats arrived and hauled my darling Wavelength Portal Refractor away along with a lifetime's supply of *Ghost-Off.*'

Dorothy gave me a worried glance.

Wuft's eyes narrowed.

'It was my former research assistant, Regus, who let them in. He was the one showing them where everything was kept!'

'So,' I asked, 'You think *he's* Dr Dust, then?'

Wuft shook his head. 'Not possible. Regus was a few sandwiches short of a picnic, if you know what I mean. He couldn't orchestrate this on his own. No. But he *could* be working for someone.'

'But you *do* think whomever Regus helped steal your research is the same person who is sucking up ghosts?'

'Without a doubt!' Professor Wuft said.

I tapped my pencil on my notepad.

'Although that still wouldn't explain the spectacles,' I thought aloud. '*Unless* Dr Dust took the Spectre-Glass from the machine and used it to have them made?'

'Who knows! Who gives a rat's rump!' Wuft sulked. His gaze drifted over his laboratory at the mouldy books and grimy flasks. 'All my research into the mysterious worlds beyond our own. Sitting here. Wasting away. And meanwhile out there some … *CHUMP* is putting my inventions to destructive, *terrible* uses.'

'We're going to stop them, Grandad,' Dorothy said firmly.

'Good luck with that,' Professor Wuft snorted, glancing at me. 'That one's far too short to have any *real* higher thinking ability. You know what they say, stubby legs …'

'Short temper,' Dorothy finished, nodding wisely.

'I'm NOT–' I began crossly, but stopped, not wanting to prove these two science giraffes right. 'We need to find Regus. And find out who he gave the machine to.'

The head rested on the armrest and the right hand scratched it.

'I'd be very careful if I were you. The type of ruthless creature that commits crimes like this won't let anything stand in their way. *Anything.*'

'So, Dr Dust stole the glass from inside that machine and had Bernard Solomon from the eyewear shop make the spectacles for him,' I panted as Dorothy and I hurried back into town.

'Yes, but we still don't know why he'd be *dislocating* ghosts,' Dorothy replied. 'We need to find out who Dr Dust really is and why he's doing it. That way we might be able to stop it.'

We were supposed to meet Mums at the *Stony Brook Autumn Markets* in the town square at the other end of the High Street. But as we approached the stretch where *Past*

Life, the Mums' antique shop, was I spotted Mum and Ma and Jude in his pram stood outside the shop.

They were talking to a policeman.

I broke into a run.

'Billy!' Mum called out in relief when she saw me. Jude let out a little dribbly wibble.

'What's happened?' I gasped, as I took in the antique shop.

All of the gramophones, carved figurines, paintings, clocks, taxidermy and vintage postcards had been ransacked. Tablecloths were clawed and globes were cracked like easter eggs. As if someone with enormously long fingernails and a bat had smashed it all up.

'Oh!' Mum gasped. 'They've even destroyed the Senzavalore Vintage Italian lamp!'

'We got a call from our neighbour, Mrs Golt,

who owns *Sew You Think you can Stitch?*,' Ma continued explaining to the policeman. 'But the windows aren't smashed, the doors are still locked and there's no sign of a break in.'

The befuddled constable made some notes.

I threw Dorothy a knowing look. As if she could read my mind, she pointed her radar discretely at the shop.

A hideous throaty yelling wailed out of her device.

'Dorothy!' Ma gasped. 'What the heck is *that*?'

'It's err ... a new type of ... synth-wave ... ambient K-Pop,' Dorothy lied, hurriedly switching it off. 'This is a radio.'

'Oh,' Mum said.

I flashed Dorothy a 'that was close!' type look.

The constable narrowed his eyes suspiciously before turning to Mums. 'It's a good thing you had CCTV cameras installed. We should be able to get a look at whoever did it.'

Oh no you won't, I thought. But the thing that scared me most was that I knew a dislocated ghost was what had made Dorothy's dad sell his shop. Now someone was trying to do the same to Mums.

I couldn't let that happen.

And as I lay in bed that night, with Hepzibah trying to rub up beside my ear, I felt more determined than ever. We'd save Mums shop. We'd save the other ghosts. And we'd stop Dr Dust in his foggy tracks.

CHAPTER 11

GHOSTED

'Allow me,' Dorothy said the next day when Ma dropped me off to meet her for milkshakes at *For Goodness Shake*.

She casually produced a twenty-pound note and handed it to the cashier.

Apparently being a top science student is quite good business. Dorothy told me that she'd won two-hundred pounds in a competition for building a gyroscopic robot wheel in the summer holidays alone.

I was happy to oblige her and asked for an 'Extra tall, caramel-melt-choc-yo-chippety-butter-bonanza milkshake. With oat milk.'

Dorothy had a small hot chocolate. It made her seem like a girl who knew what she wanted. Unlike me who could never decide and asked for everything instead.

'Let's review what we've got so far.'

I sucked as much of my milkshake up the straw as possible and pulled out my notepad.

Dorothy was pouring over an old magazine called '*The Modern Scientist*'.

I went on anyway. I was pretty sure Dorothy had a photographic memory and didn't need to keep repeating things over and over like I did.

'After Professor Wuft dies, his research assistant, Regus, who knew where everything

was, leads Dr Dust to where the portly ...
fraction ... wave-surfer-thingy–'

'Wavelength Portal Refractor 3000,'
Dorothy corrected me without looking up
from her magazine.

'Yeah. That thing. Regus leads Dr Dust
and his workers to where it was kept in the
laboratory on Swampbottom Lake. And they
steal it, along with a huge supply of *Ghost-Off*.'

'Right,' Dorothy agreed.

'Dr Dust then takes a special piece of glass
from *inside* of the machine ... spectre glass ...
and he forces Bernard Solomon, the man from
the eyewear shop, to turn the glass into a pair
of spectacles.'

Dorothy nodded.

'Then he created some other type of
machine. Or maybe *converted* the wavelength

portal thing into this contraption that he pushes around the streets at night. He vaporises the *Ghost-Off* and once the ghosts are asleep, he sucks them in and dislocates them to different places.'

'Dorothy pointed to her magazine. 'I've actually just found something very inter–.'

She stopped as the shop door opened. I glanced over my shoulder to see who it was.

Digby Knowles-Park, Maeve Binks and Dev walked in.

I thought Dev didn't even like Maeve or Digby. He thought it was hilarious when Digby told everyone he had to take a day off school because his dog was stressed about having its nails clipped.

As Maeve and Digby bustled and sank into a booth, Dev and I locked eyes. We've always

been able to communicate without talking.
It's all in the winces, smiles and rolls of the
eyes.

I gave Dev a small smile. A smile that I
was hoping said:

*Hey Dev, you OK? I'm not. Dorothy's
funny and really nice. But she's not you.
I miss you. How's baking? Oh, and I'm
really sorry for getting you into trouble.*

I thought he'd give me a smile that said:
*It's OK. I forgive you. I'll make you your
favourite brownie just to prove it.*

But instead, Dev's face was blank. And
dropping his bag into Maeve and Digby's
booth, he sat down with his back to me.

Maeve and Digby flicked their eyes
snootily at me, lifting up their menus to
cover their faces.

I turned back to Dorothy. Feeling stung. As if I wanted to cry.

Dorothy didn't seem to notice and kept talking.

'This is actually *uncanny* timing,' she said. 'Here.'

She pushed the magazine towards me, pointing at a photograph of three people. Two of them were standing proudly at the front in lab coats, one of which I vaguely recognised.

'Is that Professor Wuft?' I squinted. 'Except … he's young … and his hair's all luscious … and … well … he hasn't exploded yet, has he?'

'And look,.' Dorothy pointed at the hunched figure beside him.

'Regus Park, research assistant,' I read the caption, my eyes drifting over the photo.

It was taken in Professor Wuft's lake house laboratory. The third person in the background was wearing a boiler suit and seemed to be at work with a large mop and bucket.

'*Park.*' Dorothy drew my attention to the caption once more. 'As in Digby Knowles-Park. Regus is Digby's *dad*!'

I peered over my shoulder to where Digby, Maeve and Dev were laughing loudly, as though they were having a wonderful time. I felt a bit of anger bubbling in the pit of my stomach, like a kettle without enough water trying to boil.

'So, Digby Knowles-Park's *dad* is the one who led Dr Dust to the Professor's machine!' I whispered.

Digby let out a shrill laugh behind me and Dorothy looked up.

'Maybe Dev could find out for us?' she asked, 'Aren't you friends with him?'

'Not anymore,' I muttered bitterly as I overheard Digby boasting behind me.

'... and Mummy's booked two nail artists, foot spas, a makeover specialist and we've got the pool and we're all getting pamper packs and face masks. It's going to be PARFAIT.'

'Digby's having a party?' I asked Dorothy, as one of my nice uncooked plans poured into the frying pan inside my head.

Dorothy looked shocked. 'Only the social event of the year!'

The plan browned up a little, and in my mind, I flipped it with an imaginary spatula.

"It's his *Pamp-tastic Cucumber Slumber and Ooh-La-Spa Glow Up Soiree.'* Dorothy went on. 'He does it *every* year. For his birthday. How have you not heard about it?'

I hadn't heard about it because I'd never cared before. Digby Knowles-Park was stuck up and rude. And I'd never have *dreamed* about wanting to go to his cucumber sleepover thingy. But this was different.

'We need to get invitations,' I hissed. 'The house will be *full* of people. We can have a snoop around.'

Dorothy snorted. 'Good luck! One time when a plane flew over in the playground Digby shouted in front of everyone 'Dorothy, quick, duck!' There's no *way* he's going to invite us.'

But in my head, I took the plan off the stove and slid it onto a plate.

'Dorothy, babes.' I said pursing my lips like Maeve does to Digby. 'Watch and learn.'

* * *

'THIS is his house?' I gawped when Dorothy and I reached the Knowles-Parks' gateway twenty minutes later. 'It's HUGE!'

It was in the nice part of Stony Brook, and looked more like somewhere a villain would keep their private jet than a house.

'Are you *sure* we're not going to get into trouble?' Dorothy said as we buzzed the button at the gates.

'Trust me,' I told her. 'I know exactly what I'm doing.'

The gates swung open, and we walked towards the enormous front door.

I rubbed my eyes in preparation to make them red.

There was a yapping, scratching sound on the other side.

'JOLENE! DOWN!' came a voice.

A beautiful but sharp-looking lady with dark eyebrows and very crisp apricot-coloured lipstick opened the door holding a Chinese Crested Dog (the ones that look like a roast goose wearing a wig).

'You're not selling biscuits, are you?' the woman, who *had* to be Digby's mother demanded.

'W-w-w-ee ...' I paused for dramatic effect. 'We lost our invitaaationss ...' I sobbed putting in extra effort by collapsing onto Dorothy's shoulder. 'Digby gave us them at school. A-a-a-and ... I was so excited ... I kept it safe inside a library book ... but then ... m-m-m-my mummy returned it to the library by mistake.'

I took in a great big gasp right here and made some slimy little sounds and sniffled my nose.

Digby's mother backed away in disgust.

'Ppppleeeease let us have n-n-new ones
…' I reached out and clutched Mrs Knowles-
Park's sleeve pathetically. 'My m-m-m-mums
say I can't go unless I f-f-f-find the invitation!'

'Alright. ALRIGHT!' Mrs Knowles-Park
jerked away, her nostrils flaring. 'Here. Just
… stop … whatever it is you're doing.'

Reaching for something behind the door,
she tossed two blank invitations towards us.

'Thanks!' I said brightly and galumphed off
towards the gates, Dorothy behind me.

'Billy Hazel *Duggery*!' Dorothy held her
hand up and we high-fived so hard I could
feel it ringing for ten minutes.

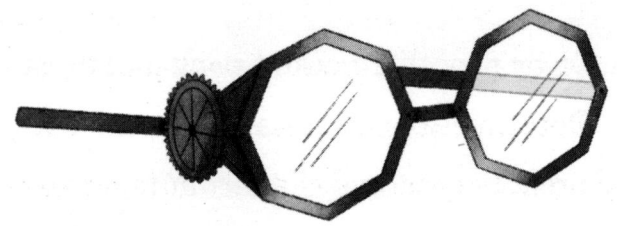

CHAPTER 12

THE PAMP-TASTIC CUCUMBER SLUMBER AND OOH-LA-SPA GLOW UP SOIREE

'Meet you out back,' I told Clifford, lifting up my spectacles for a moment so I could find where he was standing. He was busy peeping through his fingers at the Knowles-Parks' house.

Clifford nodded and drifted off.

'Nervous?' Dorothy asked as I rang the doorbell. She removed her trench-coat and my eyes nearly fell out of my head.

Dorothy Mooney was wearing what I could only describe as a sort of fancy pant suit with long silky trousers in peach pink.

'Dorothy,' I marvelled. 'You look knockout.'

'Cheers, Billy,' Dorothy said, as though people said this to her every day. 'I do love dressing up from time to time. Besides I wanted to blend in.'

Compared to Dorothy, I was dressed like something someone had entered in a scarecrow competition.

The door opened, and Maeve Binks appeared.

She had a lavender-coloured facemask on. A towel wrapped around her hair and was wearing a white bathrobe.

'I don't remember Digby inviting *you* two.'

She narrowed her eyes. 'Do you even *have* invitations?'

'Nice to see you too, Maeve,' Dorothy said, producing the invitations that Mrs Knowles-Park had given us.

Maeve scrutinised them. As if she thought they must be a forgery.

'You can put your gifts on the table by the front door,' she said grudgingly.

Gifts? I hadn't thought of gifts!

Dorothy removed an envelope from her pocket.

'It's a cheeky little gift card. From both of us,' she winked to Maeve.

Dorothy Mooney was fast becoming my personal hero.

The Knowles-Park's house had an enormous chandelier next to the stairs.

Light music was playing, and through the doorway into the back, I could see other kids from school stretched out on beach loungers and sipping fancy fizzy drinks with bits of cucumber, strawberry and mint in them. There was even a man handing out spa-slippers.

'French manicure?' a lady at a table with an assortment of nail polishes asked me.

'Absolutely not,' I said, a little too quickly.

'Blend *in*,' Dorothy said out the corner of her mouth, taking a drink from a bald waiter with dark circles beneath his eyes. He looked oddly familiar.

But I couldn't. Because Dev was stood beside Digby. Dev was really blending in. He was wearing a white bathrobe like everyone else.

Seeing him there made me want the old Dev back so badly. But I had to focus. There was more at stake than a lifelong friendship.

'Dad says that he's going to make Stony Brook into a shopping paradise,' Digby was saying to Dev as the rest of his friends surrounded him adoringly. 'There's going to be at least fifty new shops when those old stuffy ones have all been knocked down.'

Dev looked up, freezing as he caught my eye.

'I don't remember inviting you two,' Digby frowned noticing Dorothy and me.

Fortunately, at that exact moment Digby's mum appeared, wearing a celebratory silver hat, holding the Chinese Crested dog.

'Who wants *foot* spas?' she chimed.

There was an excited flutter.

Mrs Knowles-Park led everyone to an enormous pool area with a square of beach chairs, each with a foot spa at the bottom. In the middle was an enormous chocolate fondue fountain adorned with an assortment of fruit and marshmallows for dipping.

'Dev! Maeve!' Digby demanded. 'You're both next to me.'

I took a quick glance through my spectacles. Clifford was floating on an inflatable flamingo in the middle of the swimming pool.

I felt a strong grip on my forearm.

'What are you *doing* here, Billy?' Dev hissed in my ear.

'Partying,' I said, pulling away.

'I *know* you weren't invited,' Dev went on. 'I know *you*, Billy. What are you up to?'

'Can't a girl just have a gorgeous little foot spa and a nice mani-pedi, Dev babes?' I snapped.

I flounced over to Dorothy who was poking a nail polish party favour bag into the pocket of her trousers.

'We better join in,' she murmured out the corner of her mouth.

I glanced around. Everyone had lowered themselves into their loungers and were lifting the covers to their foot spas as they popped their feet into the bubbling water. We quickly did the same.

The familiar-looking waiter walked around with a small silver tray of cucumber slices and using a pair of tongs lowered them onto everyone's eyes.

Before I knew it, everyone was lying back

with their cucumber blindfolds, the fondue bubbling gently in front of us like a campfire as soothing spa music played.

I waited. Quietly. Until everyone fell silent.

Then peeling off my cucumbers, I wedged out my spectacles and pulled them on.

Clifford must have sensed what I was about to do, because he was already stood behind me.

I prodded Dorothy, who was blending in a little too well as she dozed off to the music.

We got up silently as we could and crept back into the house.

'And where might you be going?'

Mrs Knowles-Park was stood at the bottom of the staircase.

I opened my mouth, but a sudden CRASH! saved me.

We spun around.

'What the–?' Mrs Knowles-Park cried, staring in horror.

Gusts of melted chocolate were shooting out of the fondue fountain. Splattering over the sea of white bathrobes. Cucumbers flew off eyelids as gasps and shouts rang out.

I didn't need my spectacles to know what was happening.

Clifford was creating a diversion.

Mrs Knowles-Park screamed. And so did the dog.

Our classmates tried to escape from their foot spas, slipping and skidding in the puddles.

A hand smeared in chocolate slid down the window and Mrs Knowles-Parks lost it.

'KEEP THOSE FILTHY MITTS AWAY FROM MY DOUBLE GLAZING! GET AWAY FROM THE POOL! YOU'RE DESTROYING MY ZEN GARDEN!'

With a grateful glance at the fondue, we bolted up the stairs.

At the end of the luxurious hallway, we could see lamplight through the crack in the door and what looked like a desk. If we were going to dig up any dirt on Digby's dad, surely it would be in the study?

We crept along, horrified squeals and crashes still ringing out from the great fondue disaster downstairs.

I peered through the crack. The study seemed empty.

Holding our breath, we slipped inside.

The room was dimly lit, every wall covered in shelves that were stocked with important looking files.

'Billy,' Dorothy whispered.

I padded towards her. Dorothy was stood beside the large leather-topped desk, and right in the middle of it was black briefcase with brass latches.

Dorothy opened it with a *click*.

There were documents, blueprints, floorplans. We began to sift, until a familiar name appeared on a pamphlet:

BULLHAM'S DEVELOPMENTS

Investing in Tomorrow!

'They're the ones who want to build the mall!' I said. 'Digby's dad must be the one who bought your dad's shop. The one who's trying to buy Mums's antique store!'

'Can I help you?' A throaty voice came from behind us.

The two of us spun around.

I recognised Mr Knowles-Park immediately. He was small, with the sort of untidy hair that made you think someone was clever. And just a hint of something fidgety in his eyes.

'We err ...' I backed up a little, but very quickly realised that the desk was behind us, and we had nowhere to go.

'We were looking for towels!' Dorothy blurted out.

'Towels?' Mr Knowles-Parks asked with a dry chuckle. 'Are you quite sure you weren't ...'

He paused for an effect so terrifying that, for a second, I felt myself leave my body.

'*Snooping?*'

'Your wife sent us,' Dorothy explained, pretending to hunt about. 'To get some towels to clean up the mess from the fondue downstairs. Is this *not* the linen cupboard?'

'The linen cupboard is downstairs.' Mr Knowles-Parks said coldly, standing aside.

We scurried past him, my heart thumping like timpani as I felt his eyes on the back of my neck.

Downstairs chaos reigned. Big fudgy finger streaks were smeared across the walls, and two kids had jumped into the pool turning the water an unappetising milky brown.

I spotted Dev wringing chocolate out of his bathrobe which he threw down in a strop.

And his gaze fixed on me.

I couldn't help giving him a little flicker of my eyebrow. A look that said: *Serves you right. That's what you get for being friends with that lot. And you'll never be able to prove I had anything to do with it. Never! HA!*

Dev narrowed his eyes. His look said simply: *I know you had something to do with this.*

I wiggled my eyebrows brazenly. *Go on. Check the CCTV footage. You can't prove a thing.*

And with that, we slipped off.

CHAPTER 13

THE MIST AND A FAMILIAR NUMBER

Outside the Knowles-Parks', it was autumny and starting to rain, but it couldn't dampen the punch of excitement I felt when Dorothy revealed that she'd managed to sneak the Bullham's Development pamphlet out of Mr Knowles-Park's briefcase along with a handful of other documents.

We were already at the corner by the time I realised I'd forgotten about Clifford.

But when I lowered my spectacles, I found that he was tagging a few streaks behind us.

'Success?' he asked drifting to catch up.

'Thanks to you,' I grinned. 'Digby's dad is the one who's buying up the shops in Stony Brook. But before he buys them, those poor ghosts are dislocated there and go all freaky. It's *got* to be connected.'

'Yes, I know ...' Dorothy frowned at me.

'I was talking to Clifford,' I told her.

'Oh. I see,' she realised. 'As you were. Carry on.'

'The next thing we need to do is go through these documents and see if there's anything incriminating. Anything that connects the dislocated ghosts to Digby's dad and Bullham's Developments.'

'But *he* was the professor's research

assistant!' Dorothy cried out. 'He's the one who helped steal the professor's work in the first place.'

'I agree,' Clifford nodded. 'If that's not incriminating, I don't know what is!'

'But everyone thought the professor was mad,' I reminded them both. 'No one is going to believe us if we accuse Digby's dad without cold, hard evidence. We need more. There'll be *something* that connects it all. I'm sure of it.'

I took in a deep breath of evening. I could smell smoke in the air from the first fireplaces being lit, and there was a spring in my step. We were getting closer. We were going to SOLVE this. And stop Dr Dust.

I turned back to Clifford smiling at him, and through his fingers I could just see that he was smiling back.

'What happened then,' Dorothy murmured softly, 'to you and Dev? Why aren't you friends anymore?'

The question caught me off guard. But given Dorothy was just about the closest friend I had in the world at that point, I thought telling her wouldn't do any harm.

Taking off the spectacles to rub my nose, I told Dorothy what had gone down.

'Ever since we met, I've been the naughty one. And Dev's been the good one. That's just how it's always been. Good cop. Bad cop. Sort of. Which meant that if we got in trouble, usually it was me who'd landed us there.

'But our actual falling out started on the day of the Stony Brook School Fair.

'There was competition with a prize for "Best Edible Sculpture of an Animal". The only rules were that it had to be at least thirty centimetres high, and still standing when the judges came or else you were disqualified.

'Dev had made the most spectacular chameleon out of croissants, all of which he'd baked himself. It was a *masterpiece*. It even had cinnamon buns for the eyes.

'Digby, well I'm pretty sure it was Digby's mum, had made a huge peacock, out of kiwifruit cut in half with a slice of peeled melon for its beak. And it was all perched on top of a mango "egg". It looked really impressive. There were even two people with white gloves that carried it into the school hall.

'Digby looked just like his sculpture as he kept puffing out his chest and strutting around inspecting everyone else's entries.

'He let out a snort when he saw my ingenious entry, which was a stick figure of a smiling cat made out of sugar cookies. It was immediately disqualified because it only measured one point five centimeters high. I didn't care. I wanted Dev to win.

'Dev and I couldn't stop laughing. I think it was because Dev was nervous about the competition. So, I made a joke to Dev about poking the mango egg and seeing if Digby would try to peck me.

'"Billy Duggery and Dev Choudhary!" came Mr. Eugene's voice from right behind us. "'I heard that."

'Dev scurried off to get a pound from his

mum so we could play the hoopla and left me alone beside the edible sculptures. And out of sight from Mr Eugene, my little mind got to thinking.

Stupid Digby. I thought. *Stupid peacock with its stupid kiwifruit wings. Dev should win.*

'I tried to brush the thought away. I really did. But when I looked over at the sculpture, something extraordinary happened.

'The mango looked at me.

'And almost as if it had sprouted a pair of lips it started to speak.

"*Go on, Billy,*" the mango said. "*One little poke. That wouldn't hurt now, would it? No one would know.*"

"*Stop it.*" I told the mango.

"*Oh, come on. For Dev? A little prod in the right direction is all I need.*"

'And I felt myself drawn by an invisible force towards it.

"I'm like a big juicy button that you're just dying to push, aren't you?" the mango said.

'I watched as my trembling finger reached out in front of me.

'"Billy!!?" Dev appeared beside me, grabbing my arm.

'But instead of stopping, my knee-jerk reaction was to punch the mango. As hard as I could.

'It shot out from underneath the peacock like a bullet, impaling itself on the hoopla spikes.

'There was a gasp from across the hall as everyone turned. Dev and I toppled into one another. And the peacock collapsed. Into a big sloshy fruit salad on the floor.

'Digby had let out a howl of despair. And Mr Eugene had frog-marched Dev and I to his office.

'I tried to explain that it was me. All me. But Mr Eugene wouldn't hear a word of it.

'We got a bucket of detentions each. Dev was disqualified from the competition. And Digby won a big red rosette and a handshake for his sculpture because people felt sorry for him.

'It was after that that Dev stopped answering all my calls. He vanished off into the toilets at lunch whenever I tried to find him. And to my utter horror a few days later he was sitting with Digby, Maeve and their gaggle of friends at lunch.

'I knew it was my fault. But it was hurtful. Painful. As if I were a mango someone had punched across a school hall.'

'Errr … Billy?' Dorothy murmured.

'And he's still not talking to me,' I rambled on as we plodded down the street. 'I don't know what to do. He's my best friend in the world and I'm really scared that I've lost him.'

'BILLY!' Dorothy shouted.

I looked up from gazing miserably at the pavement and froze.

Down the avenue of spindly autumn trees, a poisonously thick mist was drifting straight towards us, a gaping mouth of strange smelling fog.

'Billy we should–'

'SHH!' I told Dorothy. 'Listen!'

We craned our ears.

There was a whirring chugging, growing slowly louder, as something rattled through the mist towards us.

'D-do you think,' Dorothy breathed, 'it's *him*?'

I didn't need to answer, because between the swirling cloud, we caught our first glimpse of Dr Dust and his clackety machine with the spindly nozzle.

Dorothy grabbed my fingers and squeezed, as my whole body tumbled with terror.

I could see his respirator mask with the two breathing snouts looming out from above the machine, as he headed straight for us.

We needed to run. But almost as suddenly as I'd had that thought, I remembered:

Clifford.

'CLIFFORD!' I shouted, fumbling for my spectacles.

I forced the spectacles onto my nose searching around.

'CLIFFORD!?'

But it was too late. High above us Clifford was floating, motionless, his back arched. As if he were in a dream. As if he had been lifted by the mist.

I tried to jump. Swiping pathetically at him. But it was useless.

In front of us, Dr Dust in his white hazmat suit, pinching rubber gloves and respirator mask, reached for the nozzle which was attached with a long wavy tube. Like a vacuum cleaner.

There was a squeaking of gloves followed by a hideous sucking sound as Dr Dust pointed it at Clifford and Clifford began to drift towards him, like a krill being sucked towards a whale.

I let out a shout of terror.

'CLIFFORD!'

An anger filled me, and I pummelled my feet into the ground, pounding as hard as I could towards Dr Dust.

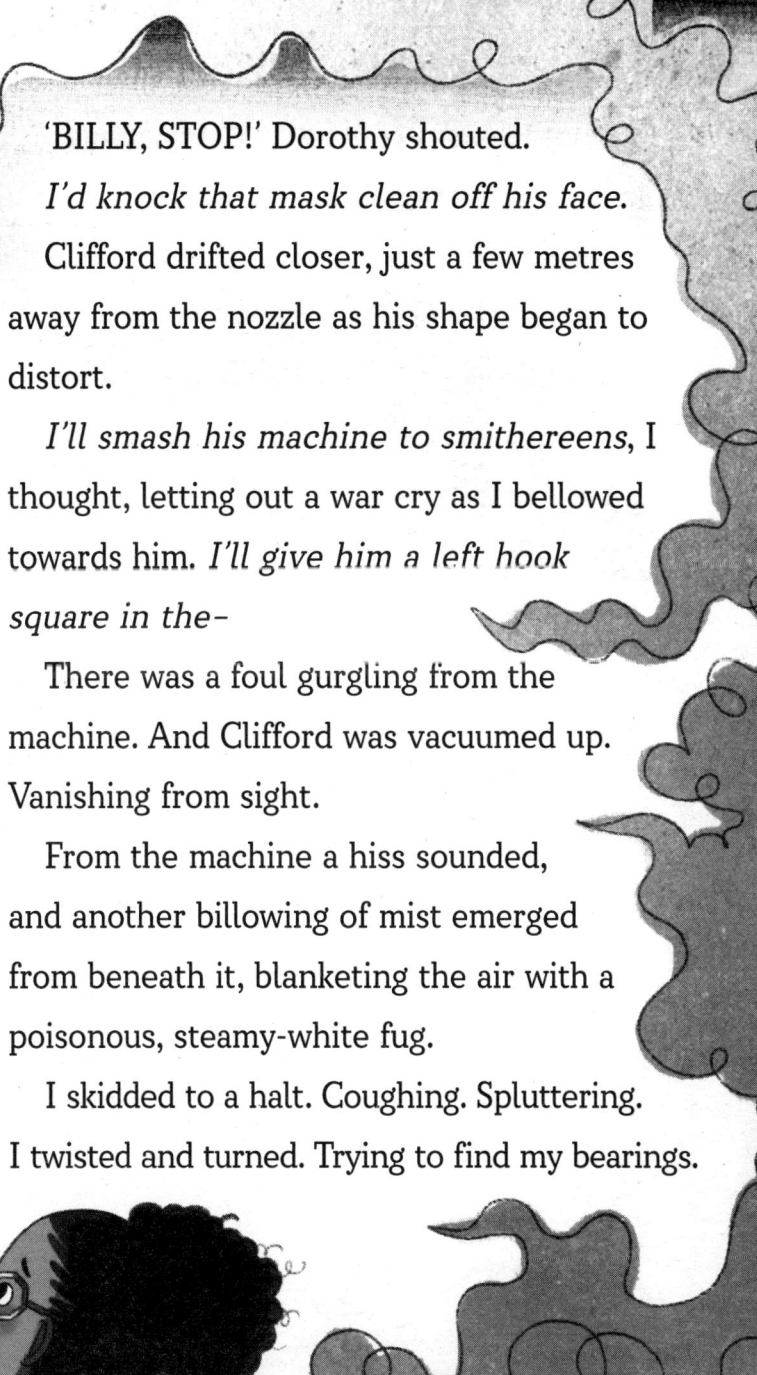

'BILLY, STOP!' Dorothy shouted.

I'd knock that mask clean off his face.

Clifford drifted closer, just a few metres away from the nozzle as his shape began to distort.

I'll smash his machine to smithereens, I thought, letting out a war cry as I bellowed towards him. *I'll give him a left hook square in the–*

There was a foul gurgling from the machine. And Clifford was vacuumed up. Vanishing from sight.

From the machine a hiss sounded, and another billowing of mist emerged from beneath it, blanketing the air with a poisonous, steamy-white fug.

I skidded to a halt. Coughing. Spluttering. I twisted and turned. Trying to find my bearings.

'*Beep! Beep!*' I could hear the machine. '*Extractor reversing!*'

'BILLY?' Dorothy appeared beside me.

As Dr Dust and Clifford with him, vanished from view I saw a number printed across the side of the machine. An incredibly familiar number:

0114 497 0998

I'd keyed in that number thousands of times on our home phone.

That was Dev's number.

CHAPTER 14

THE CONFRONTATION

'I can't BELIEVE you, Billy,' Mrs Benjamin scolded me furiously later that night. '*Poor*, poor Clifford!'

Great. Another thing that everyone thought was *my* fault.

I was slumped miserably against her fence. Sinking into the depths of despair.

'I m-m-mess everything up,' I choked back tears. 'I can't do anything right. First Dev, then the lemonade stand and now Clifford.

I've messed *everything* up.'

Mrs Benjamin sighed and lowered herself to her toadstool garden ornament beside me.

'Billy. Look at me,' she said, firmly and I looked up with a sniff.

'Do you know what I've realised now that I'm dead?'

I shook my head.

'It's what we do when we're at the bottom of a hole and feeling too scared to do anything at all that matters the most.'

I felt my eyes becoming teary again.

'Do you remember my friend Grace from Cheshire who used to come at Christmas?'

'The one who always wore matching clothes?' I asked.

'That's her.' Mrs Benjamin smiled. 'She was a gymnast. Quite the expert on the high bars. Could swing like a lemur. But I remember this one competition of hers I was a spectator at. When she spun up into the air her powdery hands outstretched ready to grasp the bar, the whole auditorium gasped. But at the very last moment, her fingers slipped, and she plummeted down landing with a splat, legs akimbo on the mats below.'

I wasn't sure what Mrs Benjamin was telling me.

'Do you know what Grace did?'

I shook my head.

'She picked herself up, brushed herself off and turning towards the spectators she took a deep and gracious bow.'

I felt a gasp inside my chest.

'And the entire audience leapt to their feet and cheered and clapped.'

Mrs Benjamin leaned in closely. 'Brush yourself off and face the music, Billy. Don't just flop down on the floor.'

* * *

The next morning a cold resolve filled me. I knew what I had to do. When I went downstairs, Ma was off to the golf course wearing her tartan golf trousers. I got her to drop me to Dev's on the way.

I'd never felt this nervous about arriving at Dev's house before. Partially because I knew he'd be extra angry with me after yesterday, but mostly because I had to confront him about what I had seen on Dr Dust's ghost extractor machine last night.

'What?' grunted Manisha when she opened

the front door wearing huge headphones.

'Has anyone told you, you look absolutely radiant this morning, Manisha?' I told her, leaning on the doorway. 'What's your secret?'

'DEVVVVV?' Manisha called, rolling her eyes.

'WHAATTT?' came his shout from the kitchen.

'BILLY'S HERE!' Manisha bellowed.

'WHAAAAT?' Dev hollered back.

'STOP SHOUTING AND GO TO THE DOOR, DEV!' Mrs Choudhary pitched in.

'IS THERE SOMEBODY AT THE DOOR?' I heard Mr. Choudhary ask.

'IT'S NOT FOR YOU!' they said all at once.

Manisha left the door wide open and frumped off.

There was a lot of commotion from down the stairs to the warehouse where they kept all their carpet cleaning equipment. Accompanied by some truly terrible singing with a jazzy jingling tune underneath it.

Mr Choudhary appeared on the stairs, wiping his hands on a cloth.

'Oh.' He frowned. 'Here to see, Dev?'

I nodded nervously.

'What's that?' I whispered pointing in the direction the din was coming from.

'*Get clean as a bean with our mean Glean Machine!*'

'That's the Mrs,' Mr Choudhary explained. 'She's recording a new jingle for the carpet cleaning business. It's going to be on TV. Voice like a nightingale she's got.'

'*And if your carpets caked in grime, get*

Choudhary's on the line!'

'Well ... maybe a nightingale being pursued by a cat.' Mr Choudhary gave me one of his wicked little grins. 'See you around, Billy!'

He wandered off. Mr Choudhary couldn't be Dr Dust. Mr Choudhary was the nicest person alive. But why was their phone number on the side of Dr Dust's ghost extractor machine?

'I told you I was–' Dev sighed as he came around the corner from the kitchen. He was wearing oven mitts, carrying an electric flour sifter and had icing sugar all over him.

'Oh,' he said bitterly. '*You.* Don't you have someone else whose life you can ruin?'

Dev sloped off. Pulling out the spectacles from my pocket, I chased him.

'This is serious, Dev.' I hissed.

When I rounded the corner into the kitchen, everything was in a state. Mixing bowls and spoons were piled up beside the sink and there was icing sugar all over the floor. Dev was usually meticulous. He ignored me as he checked whatever he was baking in the oven.

'These spectacles.' I put them on. 'They let you see ghosts. But there's someone called Dr Dust who's hurting them. Your phone number is on the side of the machine he's using. And I...'

I stopped. Trying to work out how to say it.

'Dev, if you know something, you *have* to tell me. Dr Dust has already sucked up loads of ghosts. He released one in my mums' shop. And it went all crazy. And now they're having to sell it because customers won't come.'

I leaned in for emphasis.

'We think he's hiding everything at his headquarters. So, Dorothy and I are going to break in and *stop* him.'

'Are you out of your tree, Billy?' Dev shook his head. 'What are you farting on about?!'

A heaviness came over me as Dev went back to stirring something on the stove.

At that moment, Dev's grandma who died last year hobbled through the wall and leaned over his shoulder. She threw her hands up in the air. 'If this boy thinks he's perfected my mother's milk cake recipe, he's mad. You'll knock everyone out with that much cardamom!'

'Hi Granny C,' I whispered.

'Billy!' She gasped clutching her shawl. 'You can see me?'

I nodded glumly.

'Then for goodness' sake, would you please tell this boy to go easy on the cardamom!'

'Your granny says you're putting too much cardamom in the milk cake.' I said flatly, folding my arms.

'That's not OK, Billy,' Dev said looking hurt and giving the cardamom two more shakes. 'Why would you say that?'

Granny Choudhary threw her arms in the air again and did a lap around the kitchen, vanishing for a moment as she walked through the fridge.

'She's here,' I told him. 'In this room.'

I took off the spectacles and offered them to him.

'Look. See for yourself. She's right there. And if we don't do something she might get sucked up too.'

Granny Choudhary gave me a suspicious look.

And at that moment, Dev did one of the most uncharacteristic things I've ever seen him do. Lashing out, he knocked the spectacles clean out of my hand.

The spectacles splatted into the fridge, snapped in two, and clattered to the floor.

Broken.

I dropped to my knees, picking up both pieces from where they'd landed in a small pile of icing sugar.

Dev didn't even look sorry that he'd

broken my spectacles. I could feel hot, upset waves of anger coming over me. Like I was about to cry.

But it was at that precise moment that I heard it.

'*Beep! Beep! Extractor reversing.*'

I froze. Listening. Until it came again.

'*Beep! Beep! Extractor reversing.*'

It was coming from the warehouse down the stairs.

Stuffing the two eyepieces from the spectacles into my pocket, I backed out of the kitchen as Dev turned on his electric sifter and began to scoop icing sugar into it as it billowed into a dusty cloud.

I bolted down the stairs towards the warehouse.

'Billy, what are you doing down here?'

Mr Choudhary asked, he was driving a large carpet cleaning machine with a nozzle sticking out the side. 'Didn't you find Dev?'

I froze. Every cell in my body rigid.

'That's ....' I moved around the side of the machine. A whole row of thoughts in my head suddenly slotted into place. Like books onto a shelf.

THE

DR DUST

EXTRACTOR AND
STEAM MACHINE

For maximum carpet thread penetration!
Call: 0114 497 0998 to book yours today!

'Billy?' Mr Choudhary frowned, as I stood in the middle of the warehouse gaping. 'Everything alright?'

'How many of these Dr Dust machines do you have?'

'We had two,' Mr Choudhary said. 'But we sold the other one for cheap. They let out too much steam. Becomes like a sauna when they're at full tilt!'

'Who bought it?' I blurted out.

Mr Choudhary looked at me as if I were a few peas short of a stew.

'I don't remember his name. But he has a development business. But, Billy, why is it so-'

'WHICH BUSINESS?' I asked firmly.

I didn't mean to be rude, but he needed to tell me and quick.

'I think they were called ... Bullham's Developments.'

Suddenly several more things inside my head slotted into place.

CHAPTER 15

THE PLAN

'Digby's dad must have modified the carpet cleaning machine somehow so that it could hold the ghosts,' Dorothy said that Monday lunchtime at school once I'd told her what I'd discovered. 'He must suck them up and then keep them somewhere before he relocates them.'

I'd tested out the broken spectacles using just one eye to try and find Hepzibah, and to my relief they still worked. But I had to keep the other eye covered or else everything blurred.

On the steps leading up to the art rooms, Dorothy spread out a map of Stony Brook she'd printed at the library.

'Nighthawk Tower is here.' She pointed to the far end of town. 'That's where Bullham's Developments is located. We need to break in. Find this machine and disable it.'

'What about the ghosts who have already been taken and dislocated, like Clifford?' I asked.

Dorothy rubbed her chin. 'Maybe if we can return them to their haunt of origin then they'll become their old selves again?'

'Perhaps,' I said, desperately hoping that Clifford was going to be OK.

'The hardest part is going to be getting

inside the building in the first place.'

'Quarter past eleven,' I repeated the plan we'd made. 'I'll sneak out, meet you at the front of my house. And we'll make our way from there.'

Dorothy nodded.

'I'll be the one stood in the street, that looks like they're ready to stop this ghost terrorist in their tracks.'

We grinned at each other just as the bell went to summon us back to class.

'Billy?' came Mum's voice when I pushed through the front door that afternoon. The bus drops me off at the top of our road, and I was sweaty from running all the way back.

Ma and Mum were both sat in the living room. Jude was eating a little pile of Cheeze Curls on the floor beside them. The two of them looked serious.

'Yeah?' I asked, my heart beginning to thud.

'Come sit down,' Ma said quietly, standing up and helping me to take off my rucksack.

'What's going on?' I asked.

'We …' Ma began.

'We've sold the shop,' Mum finished off. 'To Bullham's Developments.'

My heart sank into my new school shoes.

'You're not to worry,' Ma added. 'Everything's going to be totally fine. We just … won't be able to, you know … have caviar every day.'

I gave Ma's joke a pity smile.

A sick feeling sloshed around in my stomach. The Knowles-Parks had already taken my best friend and were terrorising the ghosts of Stony Brook. Did they have to take my mums' shop too?

And how could Jude be eating Cheeze Curls at such a time? I thought. But quickly remembered he was a baby and didn't really know what we were saying.

'It'll be OK.' I said, not feeling so sure myself.

Mum smiled, and Ma gave me a tight squeeze. But in the hug, I felt something else.

I ducked out from under Ma's arm.

'There's something else, isn't there?' I sensed.

Mums glanced at each other.

'Mr Choudhary called,' Ma murmured.

'And ... he was really polite ... in fact, he seemed a bit reluctant to be calling at all. But he's asked that you don't go over to their house anymore. Apparently, Dev was very upset when you left.'

I felt my heart *crack*. And I fled up the stairs to my room so I could release some tears under the privacy of my duvet.

* * *

Mums telling me about the shop and Mr Choudhary's phone call turned out to be a blessing in disguise. Because I realised that they didn't think it was odd that I wanted to spend time in my room alone.

And *that* gave me a chance to pack what I needed before quarter past eleven:

A torch, the spectacles (both halves), an eyepatch from an old Danger Mouse costume so I didn't have to hold my hand over my eye, a small Tupperware container with six leftover biscuits in it and a screwdriver in case we had to … I dunno … screw-drive something.

At about ten p.m., Mum came up to check I was asleep. I was fully dressed, with a scarf and everything and had been arranging my pillows and a pair of microwaveable slippers into a 'me-shape' beneath the duvet. It must have been convincing, because Mum smiled at the little sausage of blankets and clothes in the darkness, as I hid beneath the bed, and pulled the door shut.

Hoisting on my rucksack, I listened at the door for Mums to go to bed.

I was already wearing one eye of the spectacles with the eyepatch, and when I turned around Hepzibah was doing little loops behind me.

'We'll stop him, old girl,' I promised her. 'Don't you worry.'

Reaching out, I stroked her invisible body.

As I unhooked the latch and crept silently around the front door, I was greeted by cold air and the smell of woodfires and autumn.

It was a spectral sort of night.

'Billy!' I heard Mrs Benjamin's voice, as her glowing eyes appeared over the fence.

Crouching low, I slinked down our driveway and leapt over her faded marigolds.

'We wanted to give you this,' Mrs Benjamin told me her hands cupped. 'You'll need something to hold it inside of!'

Between Mrs Benjamin's fingers, I could see a clump of violet mist.

Unsurprisingly, Dorothy had a flask on her. It was a glass vial in fact, with a little cork stopper like you'd find in a lab.

'Ghosts' Breath,' Mrs Benjamin explained, cajoling the mysterious violet mist into the vial. 'The point where the world of the living and the world of those passed on meet. We ghosts can only interact with the very lightest of substances in your world. Like air. Just one ghost doesn't produce a great deal of Ghosts' Breath. But we had whip around and all contributed.'

From over the fence a number of heads loomed, as the ghosts of our street emerged, smiling feebly.

'Use it if you get into a sticky situation,'

Mrs Benjamin instructed me. 'Just make sure you block your ears.'

Dorothy tapped an invisible watch on her wrist.

'Onward!' Mrs Benjamin saluted us.

I took one last look back from the end of the road, all of them waving like the tails of little glowworms in the night. Their fate was in our hands. Well, their fate *and* their breath.

CHAPTER 16

NIGHTHAWK TOWER

Stony Brook was strange this late at night. The high street was one long strip of dim lamp light, with nothing but the odd cat scooping across.

Rising above everything, shaped with a sloped roof was Nighthawk Tower, silhouetted like a razor blade against the silent sky.

We ducked behind an old telephone box that smelled terrible.

'There's a guard,' I whispered.

He was in security gear, patrolling the corner of Nighthawk Tower where the double doors were.

My stomach wriggled.

'How do we get past?'

Dorothy holstered her Ecto-Plasma Wave Subsystem and narrowed her eyes.

'Using a little trick I learned from Billy Duggery.' She grinned and slipped out from behind the telephone box.

The security guard caught sight of her almost at once and turned defensively.

'Oi. Private premises. Clear off!'

Dorothy stopped right in front of him. Her lip wobbled and she let out a wail.

'I CAN'T FIND MY ... P-P-PARENTS!' she sobbed hysterically. 'AND I LOST MY STUFFED TOY D-D-DOLPHIN!'

The guard put his hands pleadingly in the air.

'OK. Shhh. Just shhhh ....'

He kept glancing around, as if he was terrified his boss was suddenly going to appear.

'Err ... where'd you last see them?'

'I WANT SNUGGLE-FIN!' Dorothy went at it again.

'Alright ... just ... just come sit inside for a second.'

Dorothy let out a spectacular bawl as the security guard beeped her inside the building with his keycard and ushered her to a stiff looking sofa in the reception area.

'Just wait there.' I heard him say. I watched as he felt his pockets. But all he could find was his walkie talkie which he spoke into.

'Errr ... Biff. You'd better get back down here. NOW.'

Dorothy went on spluttering, pausing only to give me a sturdy wink through the leaves of a potted palm.

The guard bustled off in a flap as he tried to find his phone and Dorothy leaped into action, jamming her hand on a button inside the doors.

There was a beep and they glided open.

I bolted towards her.

'Lifts are over there!' she mouthed.

The reception had stark overhead lighting and black marble floors. We skidded over to the lifts, squeaking to a halt as we ran our eyes over the long list of different offices until we came to the very top.

'Bullham Developments.' I pointed.
'31st Floor.'

From the other side of the reception, I heard footsteps, and jammed my fingers into the lift button. The numbers on the left-hand side began to light up as the lift descended towards us.

'Hello?' came the guard's voice.

I hurriedly stabbed at the button with my finger as we pressed ourselves behind an abstract sculpture, praying he didn't spot us. The light went on descending.

6, 5, 4, 3, 2, 1 ...

'Hello?' he called out again.

There was a loud ding, and the lift slid open and said, 'GROUND FLOOR!'

The guard swung around, as the two of us plunged inside.

'THIRTY-ONE!' Dorothy shouted. I jumped up, slapping the button with my hand.

The button lit up.

The doors began to lug slowly shut.

My heart pounded furiously.

Hurry up!

The guard's sweaty, panicked face appeared in the gap just as the doors closed.

But instead of wedging his fingers to stop the doors, he used his keycard. And something extraordinary happened.

The doors to the lift closed around the elastic string that the keycard was attached to. And as the lift ascended, the keycard poking out from the gap between the doors slid down the gap.

We heard a 'No, no, no! NO!' from outside the lift. The elastic string gave a stretchy twang and the keycard dropped to the floor at our feet.

'Well,' Dorothy raised her eyebrows as I picked it up. '*That* couldn't have worked out any better.'

I grinned at her, but from behind us there was a *ding*. And the doors on the opposite side of the lift glided apart.

'*Thirty-First floor. Bullham Developments.*' The lift announced.

'Is this right?' I frowned, as the two of us stepped cautiously out into the darkness.

There was no office. Just a tiny black marble room with a secure steel door that had Bullham's Developments emblazoned in sleek silver lettering above it.

'Look,' Dorothy pointed at a small touch point with a red dot of light beside the door.

Taking the keycard out from my pocket, I breathed in deeply, steeled myself and held it up next to the touch point.

There was a sharp *beep*. The light flicked from red, to *green*.

From behind the steel door there was a thudding *click*.

With a *hiss* it slid open.

Dorothy and I stepped into the long, low hanging corridor that had appeared as the lighting flickered on.

The floor was white. And the corridor had more large steel doors leading off of it, with little glass windows in them.

'It's like a lab,' Dorothy whispered.

We crept up to the nearest window which had 'Ghost Cell Culture Centrifuge' printed against the reinforced glass.

Inside, there were gleaming steel benches and apparatuses swirling.

'What do you think they're *doing*?' I asked. Dorothy just shrugged.

We crept down the cold corridor, pausing every so often to gaze through the windows where we saw more strange equipment, and cannisters bubbling with toxic colours and symbols.

'We need to hurry,' I reminded Dorothy. 'That guard will be after us.'

I was still wearing the half spectacle, but I couldn't see sign of any ghosts.

I adjusted the wavelength focus to make sure, but nothing appeared.

From beside me there was a clicking from Dorothy's headphones as she removed her Ecto-Plasma Wave Subsystem and pointed it around.

She shook her head.

'Not a peep,' she murmured.

Just then I saw a promising sign.

This door had no window in it. But it did have another touchpoint with a red light.

I tried the keycard.

Barp. It flashed red.

I let out an irritated huff. 'This has *got* to be it, right?'

Dorothy brought her nose very close to the lock and examined it.

'*WHRREEEEP! WHREEEEP!*'

The two of us leapt clean out of our skin, as an alarm sounded impossibly loudly above us. The lights flicked off, and a red siren began to flash.

Along the corridor there was a *clang*. One by one, the doors began to bolt as the facility went into lockdown.

I scrambled for my pockets, my fingers fumbling with the vial containing the Ghost's

Breath Mrs Benjamin had given me.

With no idea what I was doing, I smashed the glass vial against the touch point. The misty purple substance floated for a moment in the air, before sucking into the touchpoint like steam down a sewer vent.

'COVER YOUR EARS!' I yelled to Dorothy as we ducked.

There was an explosive *puff* of ghostly air that knocked us off our feet, followed by a sharp *bang* that was halfway between a yelp, a scream and a hammer hitting a washing machine.

And with a clatter, the door shot open.

'GET IN!' I bellowed, pushing Dorothy through.

We scrambled, our feet sliding on the polished white floor.

227

There was a magnetic slam as the door thundered shut behind us, and from the other side we heard the bolt thunder across.

My elbow was throbbing from where I'd knocked it against the doorway.

But we were *in*. And what we could see in the flickering red light was stranger than anything I'd expected.

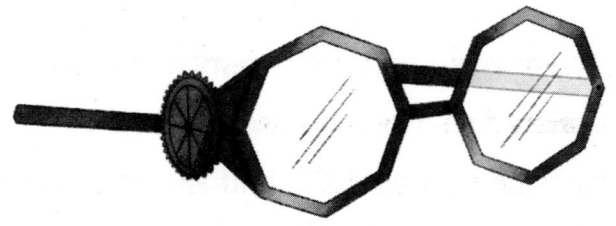

CHAPTER 17

THE WAVELENGTH PORTAL REFRACTOR 3000

'It's like ... a library.' I squinted as my eyes adjusted to the flashing darkness. Rows and rows of steel shelves reached into the distance.

Dorothy let out a little groan and climbed achily to her feet.

She flicked a switch on her Ecto-Plasma Wave Subsystem from 'Headphone' to 'Speaker', and pointed it in front of us as her radar gun began to *click*.

I rummaged in my backpack until I found my torch and together, we hunted along the shelves. But there were no books, only ...

'Metal cannisters,' Dorothy murmured examining the silver objects in neat rows.

'What do you think they're for?' I asked.

Dorothy pointed the nose of her gun at the nearest canister.

The clicking intensified, before transferring into a staticky radio sound and a foggy voice emerged from the speaker.

'*Let meeeee out!.*'

Dorothy pointed her gun at a different canister.

'*Where ammmmmmmm I?? HELLLLLLLP!*'

'Dorothy,' I breathed, reaching out and selecting one of the metal canisters. 'You don't think ...'

I held the object up to the light.

There was a printed label along its side:

Hotel maid with mop – died 1978
(specimen not fit for relocation)

I read the next one.

Jazz Nun with saxophone – (specimen to
be centrifuged) – Captured: 21st April.

And another.

Colonel with half mustache – (specimen
ready for relocation) - Captured: 9th July.

'They're ghosts,' I quivered. But Dorothy
had noticed something.

'Holy Promethium,' she breathed.

A vast machine stretched across one entire side of the room. At either end there seemed to be a door-sized opening with yellow and black flaps. Like the scanner your luggage goes through at the airport. And between each of them, was a complex looking network of pipes and tubes, thrusting and doglegging.

'This must be ...'

'Your grandad's machine,' I finished, as we gazed up at the monster of flickering metal and glass.

'The Wavelength Portal Refractor 3000,' Dorothy murmured in wonder. 'The machine which he hoped would transport objects *between* wavelengths.'

'But what would Regus Knowles-Park need this for?'

'Perhaps,' came a sharp cold voice
from behind us, 'he was merely hoping
to return the research back to the person
whose genius gave birth to the idea in the
first place!'

We spun around. In the gushes of steam
and flickering red light we saw a haunting
and familiar silhouette.

A white hazmat suit. Long rubbery fingers.
The respirator mask.

'D-d-Dr Dust,' Dorothy quavered, grabbing
my fingers.

'W-w-we know who you are!' I shouted, as
we backed away. 'And we know what you're
doing!'

'Oh, I'm sure you know the *what*,' the
figure laughed. 'But I don't think you've any
idea of the *who* or the *why*.'

My hand quivering, I raised the torch slowly to the masked face.

There was a sucking intake of air.

My eyes flitted around until they rested on a metal stool beside one of the benches.

My other hand snatched it up.

'Show yourself!' I shouted, Dorothy and I huddling together. 'Or I'll ... I'll ...'

I angled myself towards the Wavelength Portal Refractor.

'I'll smash this machine! I'll SMASH IT!'

I raised the stool high in the air.

Dr Dust paused. I'd spooked him. The yellow gloved hands reached for the mask. There was another sucking intake. The mouthpiece slid away.

And Mrs Cressida Knowles-Park, her eyes snakish and piercing, came into view.

'You ...'

'Me,' she sneered.

'But how–' I began hopelessly, my head spinning.

'Because it was *me*!' she snapped. 'Your grandfather and my porridge-headed fool of a husband thought they ruled the world of paranormal science. They boasted vainly that they'd come up with the idea for a machine which could move objects between wavelengths. After all, how could someone as lowly as their humble hazardous waste cleaner know *anything* about the delicate and undiscovered worlds that sat alongside our own?'

'It was *you*!' I cried out, remembering the magazine Dorothy had shown me, *The Modern Scientist*. 'You were in the background of the photo!'

'For years those two took every brilliant idea I ever had and claimed it as their own. They were so absorbed in chasing glory that they never even noticed me. But I waited. Patiently. Until the time was right. And I made sure no one would ever take their experiments seriously *ever* again.'

'*Ghost-Off!*' I remembered. 'The perfume!'

'Oh, it worked alright. Lulling ghosts to sleep. But what was the point of something like that if you couldn't prove that there were ghosts living alongside us in the first place?'

'So, it was you who *stole* the Spectre-Glass from Professor Wuft's machine!' Dorothy fumed. 'You made everyone think he was a laughingstock!'

'It worked better than I could have ever imagined,' Mrs Knowles-Park smirked.

'I married that fool, Regus, securing myself a now loyal footservant who would assist me without question until my revenge was exacted, and the world knew my name.'

Mrs Knowles-Park took a step towards us. But I brandished the metal stool above the machine again and she raised her hands defensively. She *really* didn't want the Wavelength Portal Refractor to be broken.

'Why the carpet cleaner?' I demanded, trying to buy us some time.

'I needed something that could simultaneously emit *Ghost-Off* in a gaseous form, as well as suck up the ghosts once they were asleep. With a little adapting, the carpet cleaner was perfect. Once they were captured in their osmium-lined capsules, a quick spin in our specimen centrifuge and a few micrograms of pure helium to latch onto their ghost particles, scrambled them up and stretched out those ghoulish features. Then we'd relocate them; releasing the haunting apparitions you would have seen in your parent's shops.'

I glanced behind us. We were cornered, with no way out.

'But why were you trapping all those ghosts in the first place?' I asked. 'Why are you dislocating them?'

Mrs Knowles-Park removed her gloves and examined her long-manicured nails.

'Despite what anyone ever tells you, you can never get anything done in this world without the one thing that makes it turn.'

'Inertia?' Dorothy asked.

'MONEY!' Mrs Knowles-Park spat. 'We released dislocated ghosts into shops so they would send the owners packing. Then we would swoop in, ready to buy them up and knock them down for as low a price as possible, building malls and apartments in their place.'

I thought of Mums' little antique shop. They'd worked for it their whole life. And now *she* owned it. This evil, vengeful woman.

I felt like a kettle as my blood boiled.

'It's brilliant, really,' Mrs Knowles-Park sighed. 'Because no matter how hard-topped, sensible and pragmatic they are, there is one thing that everyone on earth fears.'

I tried desperately to think of a way out, glancing hopelessly for something around the room I could use.

'Things they cannot explain,' Mrs Knowles-Park finished. 'Which is why I'm sure your parents, girls, will move away from Stony Brook forever, when they cannot for the life of them find where their children vanished off to.'

There was a piercing hiss from behind us, followed by another alarm. The Wavelength Portal Refractor 3000 whirred into motion.

'Toby?' Mrs Knowles-Park called.

A pair of arms grabbed Dorothy. It was the sweaty man who had buried the spectacles behind antique shop. The man I'd recognised at Digby's birthday party.

'Toby was using those spectacles to try to locate the areas of Stony Brook with the densest ghost population, when he became a little too spooked and tried to get rid of them.' Mrs Knowles-Park narrowed her eyes. 'But he's since paid for the mistake he's made.'

Before I could do anything, Toby snatched Dorothy's radar gun and flung it across the room, where it shattered against one of the shelves. And with a shove, he pushed Dorothy into the door-sized opening at one end of the machine.

I tried to stagger forwards, my feet slipping on the shiny floor. But Toby slapped a small white button. With a hiss, a glass door slammed shut over the opening. Dorothy was trapped. And the machine was beginning to whirr.

I pointed the metal stool at Mrs Knowles-Park. I could smash the machine. But what if it exploded or something and hurt Dorothy?

'HELP!' Dorothy pounded on the glass. BILLY!'

'Drop your weapon and handover the Spectracles,' Mrs Knowles-Park said. 'Or with the press of a button, your friend will be transported to another wavelength. Never again to be seen.'

Panic swirled like a hurricane inside of me.

'HERE!' I tossed the stool aside so that it skidded to a halt against the wall. Snatching one half of the spectacles off my face, I dug hurriedly in my bag for the other. 'Take them!'

I threw them to Mrs Knowles-Park, who caught them both in one hand.

'JUST LET MY FRIEND GO!'

Mrs Knowles-Park took a deep, venomous breath. 'Oh, silly girl,' she sneered. 'There's one thing that you learn when you clean up hazardous waste for so many years: don't leave *any* traces.'

I felt an arm scoop around me. Holding me back.

'Hello, Cressida, my luscious raindrop.'
Mr Knowles-Park's feeble voice came from
behind me.

I tried to yank free, kicking backwards as
hard as I could.

'Hit the button, Toby,' Mrs Knowles-Park
sneered, and Toby raised his hand poised to
press it.

But from over by the door, I heard voices.
'Get BACK HERE, LAD!'

The security guard skidded into the lab, as
somebody ducked under his arm. There was
a familiar, belly-wrenching howl as a small,
mouse-like shape collided headfirst straight
into Toby's stomach, knocking him over.

'Billy!' the mouse-like shape shouted. And
almost at once, I felt teary.

It was Dev.

CHAPTER 18

HULLO

I kicked Mr Knowles-Park clean in the shins and barrelled forwards, slapping my hand against the OPEN button on the Wavelength Refractor. There was a gush of air and Dorothy toppled out, hugging me with all her might. She was safe. Well, safe-er.

'I didn't believe you, Billy,' Dev gabbled. 'I thought you were just using it as a way to talk to me again. But ... well ... I'll tell you later.'

I squeezed Dev's hand.

'The police are on their way!' Dev shouted.

Mrs Knowles-Park flared her nostrils. 'Who do you think they're going to believe? Three fanciful children? Or a respected, prosperous member of the Stony Brook community. It's *you* who are trespassing here.'

'We'll prove it,' Dev said defiantly. 'We'll show them Billy's spectacles.'

He turned to me.

'Billy ... you *do* have the spectacles, right?'

My tummy tightened.

'POLICE!' came a shout from the door. There was torchlight through the fog, and flashing silhouettes.

'Over here, officer!' Mrs Knowles-Park called out, adding a tone of distress to her voice.

'We had a report of suspicious activity!' the officer called.

'A break in, in fact, officer.' Mrs Knowles-Park said, as if butter wouldn't melt. 'These three.'

The police officers, five of them, picked their way over the remains of Dorothy's shattered radar gun.

'SHE'S LYING!' I shouted in panic. 'They're doing experiments up here. Experiments on ghosts!'

'Ah, Mr and Mrs Knowles-Park,' the first officer nodded politely. 'Apologies for the intrusion.'

'Quite alright, officer,' Mrs Knowles-Park said graciously.

A fury stormed through me. Mrs Knowles-Park was right. Who was going to believe us?

'It's those three,' Mrs Knowles-Park pointed.

'They barged past our security guard and broke in here with some monstrous story about ghosts!'

'Right,' the first officer said, waddling towards us. 'Come on you three!'

'SHE'S LYING!' I shouted. 'They're trapping ghosts and using them to scare people out of their houses and shops so they can buy them. Who knows, they might have your mad uncle, your wacky grandma, your eccentric aunt trapped here in those canisters ready to turn them into monsters!'

'What did I tell you, officers?' Mrs Knowles-Park said. 'I'm afraid this is clearly a case of lax parenting and too many YouTube videos. These poor young people get so swept up in it that they begin to spout all sorts of nonsense!'

'That's it. Nice and easy,' another officer

said as they ushered us towards the door.

But Dev shouted with all his might, 'I CAN PROVE IT!'

Everyone fell silent.

'Please,' he begged softly, taking off his rucksack.

The lead officer looked to Mrs Knowles-Park for instruction, and she shrugged with a pitiful sneer.

The lead police officer sighed, 'How?'

Dev yanked at the zip of his rucksack and pulled out an electric sifter.

I prayed that he wasn't about to try baking a batch of flipping muffins.

'Billy, Dorothy,' he turned to us and swallowed. 'I need you to find me a *ghost*.'

I glanced at Dorothy, my heart thumping. 'Clifford,' I said.

The two of us raced towards the shelves.

Mrs Knowles-Park began to look uncomfortable.

'Actually, officer.' she said sweetly. 'On second thoughts, I wouldn't want to keep you from your important wor–'

'It's the reason I realised Billy wasn't lying,' Dev panted, hunting along the wall until he found a switch.

Dorothy and I hunted between the shelves, our eyes skipping over the nametags on the canisters.

Farmer – flattened by pig

Lifeguard stuck in blow-up ring

Chimney sweep trapped in chimney

Until just when my heart had sunk hopelessly into my toes, I saw it:

Boy flung from Ferris Wheel – specimen ready for relocation

'GOT HIM!' I shouted, snatching up the canister.

I hurried over to where Dev was setting up his sifter. He switched it on and began to feed sugar through the sieve.

'I was using this,' he panted, 'and it was grinding the icing sugar up too much and making the powder go everywhere, and some of it settled on the ground ... and ... when I looked down, I could see ... footprints. Footprints that definitely weren't mine. And definitely weren't Billy's. And then I asked

Granny if she was there. And do you know what happened next?'

I shook my head. Just feeling glad to have Dev back on my side.

'She wrote "TOO MUCH CARDAMOM",' Dev sniffed. 'And I knew it was her. The icing sugar must have been so fine that she could *move* it somehow.'

Dev stepped back, a fine white powder now coating the glassy floor.

Mrs Knowles-Park looked terrified. 'Officer, I really think–'

But before she could finish, I'd lifted both latches on either side of the metal canister.

There was a hiss as the gases inside it released.

As I poured out the invisible contents, everything fell deathly silent.

Nothing happened.

My heart thumped like crazy. I could feel a pulse in my eyeballs.

Maybe we were too late? Maybe Clifford had already been so terribly dislocated that he didn't know who he was anymore.

'See?' Mrs Knowles-Park snapped,

sweeping across the room. 'Nonsense. Now if you don't mind officers, I'd rather like t–'

'LOOK!' the curly haired police officer shouted.

My whole body prickled with triumph.

As everybody leaned in, a very Clifford-ish word appeared in the icing sugar:

CHAPTER 19

FRIENDS?

It turned out that dislocating Clifford and adding helium hadn't made any difference. Because he died mid-flight, there was nowhere he could really be dislocated *to* except indoors. So that's exactly what had happened.

I introduced him to Dev through one of half of the spectacles. Dev was a little apprehensive at first, but after a while he got used to him.

Mrs Knowles-Park wailed and kicked as the police handcuffed her, Mr. Knowles-Park and Toby the sweaty man.

'Don't worry, my beautiful evening plum!' Regus comforted her feebly. 'I'm sure everything will work out for the best!'

'HOW could this POSSIBLY work out for the best, you prat, Regus!' she yapped.

The police called the mums, and Dev's and Dorothy's parents. And we sat wrapped in blankets on the step outside Nighthawk Tower waiting for them. Clifford stayed upstairs to comfort the dislocated ghost of an exhausted pet ferret that had escaped from its canister and run fifty circles around the room, when one of the police officers accidentally knocked it off the shelf.

I felt so tired as I waited for Mums that

my eyes were sore. All I could think about was stumbling into bed and falling asleep as soon as I hit the pillow.

Heck, I could have fallen asleep on the step.

Dorothy's parents arrived looking shaken and she trotted over to where they were speaking with the lead police officer.

Dev was sat to my right, gazing down at his feet.

I didn't know what to say. So, I tried to keep the momentum of the night going.

'Did you see Mrs Knowles-Park getting loaded into the police van?' I grinned. 'She looked like a–'

Dev turned and stared at me.

'Like *what*, Billy?' he croaked. 'It isn't funny, you know. What about Digby?

He'll probably have to go live with his grandparents now.'

Cold dread crept over me. Why couldn't Dev have just gone back to being his old self?

'I realise you weren't lying about the ghosts,' Dev admitted. 'But I can't be like you all the time, Billy.'

'I'm so, so sorry about the fruit sculpture thing,' I whispered.

'It's not just that,' Dev prodded a bottle cap in the gutter with the tip of his trainer. 'When you just do stuff and don't think about how it effects other people it makes me feel like ... like you don't even care ... about me. You're funny. And people think you're cheeky. But I'm not ... I'm way more of a goody-too-shoes than–'

'No, you're NOT!' I snorted.

'YES,' Dev said firmly. 'I am.'

'Dev?' I heard Mr and Mrs Choudhary's voices and Dev stood up.

He looked back at me.

'See you around, Billy.'

I watched as he hugged his mum and dad.

'Errr ... I think these might be yours?' The curly-haired police officer was cradling the remains of Dorothy's Ecto-Plasma Wave Subsystem as well as the two halves of the spectacles. He laid them on the footpath beside me and put his hands on his hips awkwardly.

'So ... those cannisters upstairs ...' he chuckled nervously. 'They're filled with ... *ghosts* you say?'

I wasn't really listening. Because around

me and inside me everything felt broken.
Dorothy's radar, the Spectracles, and my
heart.

CHAPTER 20

BETTER

The following few days I was given extra special treatment by Mums. Especially when the police informed us that the sale of the antique shop hadn't in fact gone through. Because of a something in the Theft Act of 1968 called 'Obtaining property by deception'. They were pretty blown away when they found out everything that had happened. And after I showed Ma through one half of the spectacles that Mrs Benjamin was in fact still our neighbour, she had to go down to the driving range to swing her golf clubs and get the shock out of her system.

We spent a full day all together, just me, Mums and Jude sweeping, straightening, tidying and dusting at the antique shop. Soon it looked back to its old self with just a few less antiques, which Mum said needed to happen anyway because no customer should have to hold their breath as they navigated through a shop.

I quite enjoyed the extra little '*You OK, Pumpkin?*'s and the '*Give Billy that nice big square of chocolate*' but inside I still felt absolutely miserable. It wasn't even what Dev had said to me afterwards that kept replaying in my head. It was the memory of how happy I'd felt when I'd seen him coming to save us.

It felt empty now that it no longer meant what I thought it had.

'You look a bit peaky, Billy,' Mrs Benjamin said the next day as I pruned her climbing roses under strict instruction.

I pecked irritably at a thorny little branch.

'It's Dev,' I muttered. 'We used to be friends. Best friends. But now we're not.'

'Ah,' Mrs Benjamin said, blowing furiously at some cobwebs gathering over her windowsill. 'Whose fault is that?'

I snipped irritably again.

'Mine,' I murmured. 'He says I'm too pushy and make him do things he doesn't want to do. And that I do things without thinking about other people.'

'And *do you*?' Mrs Benjamin asked,

looking a little worried at how cavalier I was being with the sheers.

'Yeah,' I bumbled. 'I suppose.'

'Then I'm sorry, Billy, but I just don't see the problem,' Mrs Benjamin said. 'Put your pride aside and tell Dev that you'll learn to listen more.

'And *run*. Run like the wind,' she told me, as I tried to gaze at my shoes. 'Not everyone gets the chance to call someone their best friend you know, Billy. So if I were you, I'd grab onto it with both hands. My whole life would have been entirely different without my friend Grace. True friends don't just accept you for who you are, they're brave enough to help you become who you're meant to be.'

Tossing aside the sheers, I leapt over Mrs

Benjamin's garden as she shouted, 'WATCH THE HOLLYHOCKS!' and bolted down our street, crisscrossing Stony Brook until exhausted and completely pooped out, I knocked furiously on Dev's front door.

'Why are you *always* here?' Manisha huffed, but I didn't have enough oxygen to try charm her. Barrelling past, I burst into the kitchen.

Dev was leaning on the counter in his apron, watching someone who had to be Granny Choudhary writing something about a recipe in a field of powdery icing sugar.

'Oh, it's two and a *half* cups,' he was saying. '

I doubled over, wheezing, and Dev turned.

'Bulldozer …' I panted.

'What? Where?' Dev asked.

I held up my hand for him to hang on just a minute.

'Me ...' I gasped. 'I'm sorry. For being a bulldozer. I don't think about you when I do things. You're my best, truest friend. And someone very recently told me that best friends don't just accept us, they make us even better. And ...' I felt my eyes becoming red and teary. 'I just miss you. So much.'

Dev stood awkwardly upright.

'Ever since we stopped talking,' he rasped. 'I haven't been able to concentrate. I couldn't get recipes right, the kitchen's always messy and everything I made tasted like ... like something was missing.'

I hoped against hope.

'Sometimes you *are* a bulldozer, Billy,' Dev continued. 'But sometimes it's a good thing.

Like that baking competition you forced me to enter, and I won all those free baking moulds? Or that time we went to the lake, and you said I *had* to get in, even though I didn't want to, but when I did, we found that stone shaped exactly like a tooth?'

I nodded, feeling a little sob coming up my throat. It was so nice to just be talking to Dev. Tazzy-Dev. Devilled Egg. Dev.

'After everything that happened, I started to realise that part of the reason I was so angry was because...'

Dev had a little sob at the back of his throat too.

'Because I thought I'd messed it up with my best friend. And I didn't know if I was going to get her back.'

'I thought I'd lost you forever,' I whispered.

Dev and I hugged. And had a little cry together. Then halfway through crying we started laughing. And we couldn't stop laughing because we were both so snotty and teary. We were rudely interrupted by Manisha shouting.

'BILLY! PHONE!'

I picked up the landline in the Choudhary's kitchen and put it on speaker.

'Billy?' came Mum's voice. 'The police are here. They need you. And Dev and Dorothy.'

Dev and I gave each other a puzzled frown.

I called Dorothy then Dev and I pegged it back to our house. Dorothy was already there, waving at us like a windmill. She's brilliant. Ma made tea, and all of us sat around the living room as the officer explained.

'You see…' he began. 'The problem is now that the case is closed, we've been left with all these cannisters from Nighthawk Tower. And none of the officers want to go near them. Bit jittery at the idea of handling … poltergeists and … spirits and that sort of thing. So …'

We all held our breath.

'I don't suppose …'

'Yes?' I asked.

'I don't suppose you kids would be up for getting the ghosts back to where they should rightfully be?'

Me, Dev and Dorothy glanced at one another.

'We would pay you,' the officer added.

I looked pleadingly at Ma and Mum.

'Well, on the condition that Dorothy and Dev's parents are OK with it ...' Ma began, 'And ONLY if all homework is done ... And with the proviso that if it starts to affect your schoolwork, then you'll have to stop ...'

Ma glanced at Mum.

'Then, OK.'

My fist balled up in triumph. Sometimes I have the best Mums.

I designated myself as spokesperson for the group.

'One pound ... twenty. Per ghost,' I negotiated.

'DONE!' The police officer took a relieved swig of tea. 'You know ... you three ought to get a name for yourselves. Like the Ghostbusters.'

It could have just been my imagination, but as the three of us looked at one another, it felt like we all had the same idea at once … and it wasn't to open a non-homemade lemonade stand.

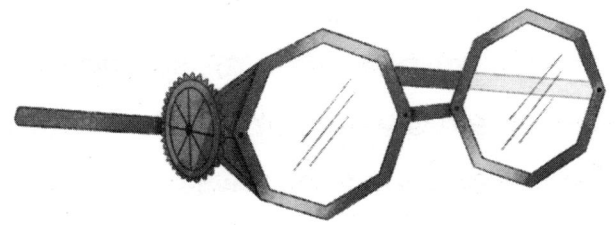

CHAPTER 21

THE AGENCY BEGINS

That Saturday, I woke up extra early, packed both parts of the broken spectacles, a little something Mum had helped me make for Dev, a note pad, pen, an armful of snacks, and headed out to the start of the trail that led to Swampbottom Lake.

The air was flooded with autumn smells, and a thick cloak of mist wove between the honey-coloured trees like wafts of cotton candy.

I popped on one half of the spectacles just in time to see Clifford run straight through Dev, who looked surprised when he let out a yawn.

'It didn't take much to fix it, actually,' Dorothy told us turning her Ecto-Plasma Wave Subsystem in her hands. 'It gave me a chance to revisit some of the hardware and I managed to condense it even more.'

Her radar was now fitted over her forearm and had a Bluetooth transmitter that sent the signal to her wireless earphones.

Pulling aside the creeping weeds that had grown up over Dorothy's grandad's front door, we crept into the crumbling, old lake house.

'I know it's not much,' Dorothy told Dev, as we elbowed through some cobwebs. 'But it could be our headquarters.'

'It's *perfect.*' I said, putting my hands on my hips and scanning around.

Dorothy wandered off, looking for Professor Wuft's ghost.

'Here,' I told Dev, holding out one half of the broken spectacles and the little gift I'd got Mum to help me make for him. 'Dorothy has her Subwave plasma listening thing, I have the other half of the spectacles ... you need something.'

Dev unfurled the eyepatch with a silver octagon embroidered on it. When you wore it along with the half spectacle, it made it look like one full pair of glasses.

'You've always given me half of everything,' I told him. 'Now it's my turn.'

Dev gave me one of his Devviest grins.

There was a hurried knocking on the door

behind us. I opened it.

'A-a-are you, Billy, Dorothy and Dev?' the courier asked, a sheen of sweat covering his forehead.

'Uh-huh,' I nodded.

'Would you … err …' he coughed apologetically. 'Would you mind helping me to move the delivery? '

'You don't like the idea of handling ghosts,' I said, rolling up my sleeves. 'Don't worry, I totally get it. Leave it with us.'

Once the courier van had roared off in a terrified splatter of mud, we set up a brilliant system. Well. Dorothy did. She was in charge of the science element, which involved pumping the cannisters through some cryogenic piping. Apparently, this would make the ghosts liquify, which sounded gross, but it allowed Dorothy to remove something called 'crude helium'.

I asked her if this was the same stuff that went into party balloons. And she said, 'sort of'. So then I asked her if we could use the excess helium to do funny voices. But she said, 'it wouldn't be appropriate'.

Once Dorothy had done her bit, she'd pass the cannister on to me and Dev. We'd open it in an enclosed fumes cupboard so that the ghost couldn't escape. Clifford then acted as ghost liaison, convincing each of the discombobulated phantoms to pass on their information. Dev and I filled out a form, labelled the canister, and puffed it with a spray of *Ghost-Off.* To lull the unsuspecting phantom back inside like a spider into a jar where they could sleep until they were relocated to their haunt of origin.

A few hours later, just as we persuaded a particularly ferocious old lady with a gaping mouth and a mean little zimmer frame back into her canister, I heard the letter flap on the door go *clap*!

A letter had appeared on the doormat. And it was addressed to:

> *The Agency for Ghost Displacement*
> The Old Lakehouse
> 1 Swampbottom Lane
> Stony Brook

'I err ... may have updated our address online,' Dorothy admitted, and then added hurriedly, 'we can change the name ... I was just ... trying something out.'

I sliced the envelope's tongue open and pulled out a scrawled note on lined yellow paper.

Dear Agency for Ghost Displacement, I'm not sure if this is something you can help me with, but I saw an advertisement of yours in the Stony Brook Journal and I'm desperate-

'Dorothy,' I paused. 'Did you put–'

'It was just a small ad,' she confessed. 'I thought there might be other people out there that need help...'

Dev grinned, and I kept on reading.

I work as a park warden for the Stony Valley National Park, and every year tourists come for miles around to see our spectacular blooms of bluebells in Rookwillow Woods. But for the past three years we've been plagued by strange sightings of a four-legged creature from our visitors, and our staff have continually found the bluebells shredded to pieces.

We've tried everything. We've even set up cameras overnight. But so far, our every attempt to uncover what is happening has been without success.

Which is I'm writing to you.

If this sounds like something you could help us with, please call our office and ask for Mary, that's me.

Very warmest wishes,

Mary Sixsmith

'A dislocated ghost, do you think?' I asked.

'Doesn't sound like it ...' Clifford said darkly. 'Especially if people can sometimes *see* it.'

Professor Wuft's head butted in, 'Well, that's patently obvious. There's more out there to worry about than just *ghosts*, you know!'

We stared at one another.

'Wh-what do you mean 'more to worry about'?' I asked.

'Oh, for goodness' sake!' Wuft scoffed, 'Do you *really* mean to tell me you weren't just the slightest bit curious what that adjustable wavelength dial on the side of your spectacles was for?'

My fingers reached up instinctively and touched it, as my head thrummed.

'Hang on,' Dorothy shook her head. 'You're saying there are *other* wavelengths? Not just the ghost one?'

Wuft slowly nodded.

'Well then … what's in them?'

Wuft's head drifted off towards his desk, and we hurried after him as he circled around what appeared to be an empty jar.

'See for yourself,' Wuft said dreamily, gazing into the empty cylinder of glass.

Dev and I began hurriedly twisting our dials.

'In other wavelengths,' Wuft's voice came from Dorothy's subsystem. 'All manner of strange and invisible things as yet unknown to science lurk.'

I could see the lenses in my spectacle shifting, until just when I thought I'd turned the dial a full rotation, there was a sudden glow of poisonous green light in front of me.

I stopped.

Dev gaped. He could see it too.

It was swirling about inside the jar, a tiny blob, with what appeared to be two limp arms drooping out from underneath.

I crouched beside it, mesmerised, my fingers reaching out.

'Err, I wouldn't get–' Wuft began.

A mouth stretching right across the eyeless lump reared open, letting out a high-pitched *scream* that made my ear drums rattle.

I stumbled backwards, my heart flying up into my throat.

The shrieking lump threw itself against the glass, hammering with its tiny fists, trying furiously to escape.

'Wh-what the heck is *that*?' I panted.

Dev gave Dorothy a turn of his spectacle.

'A nightmare?' Wuft shrugged. 'A portal? A banshee's death scream? Who knows.'

'H-how did you find it?' I asked, bewitched.

'Many years ago, it escaped during one of my experiments from an unknown wavelength into our own.'

There was another maddened howl from the lump.

'Impossible to say what else could be out there,' Professor Wuft said, his voice full of mystery. 'Ghouls and strange beasts? Wraiths made of mere shadow? Why, these are the things which haunt the shallow spaces beneath our beds. The stuff of which our dreams are woven. *Spectral* stuff.'

My pulse began to quicken in the most delicious way. I was terrified, and yet my whole body thumped with excitement.

From over near the window, there was a grating *ringing* from the rusty old telephone.

Dev and I turned to Dorothy.

'I *may* have also updated the telephone number,' she coughed bashfully.

'Then I think we better update our name too,' Dev grinned. 'Maybe it could be like an agency?'

My pulse quickened some more.

'Yes,' I said, tenting my fingers. 'An agency … for spectral stuff.'

Check out Sweet Cherry's other great adventure novels!

A hot summer in Australia brings one young girl face-to-face with the climate crisis.

Luckily, you're never too young to save the world ...

An underground adventure involving robbers, secret passages, old friends — and true courage!

And look out for the next spooky story in Halpin's exciting new series ...

COMING AUTUMN 2025!

View the full range at
www.sweetcherrypublishing.com

Sweet Cherry